WHITE SPACES
MISSING FACES

Why Women of Color Don't Trust White Women

CATRICE M. JACKSON

International Best-Selling Author

Published by Catriceology Enterprises.

Omaha, NE | United States of America

FOR INFORMATION CONTACT:
Catrice M. Jackson, M.S., LMHP, LPC
Global Visionary Leader of the Awakened Conscious Shift, International Speaker and International Best-Selling Author.

Online ordering is available for all products at:
www.shetalkswetalk.com
www.awakenedconsciousshift.com
www.catriceology.com

ISBN-13: 978-0-9838398-3-5(Catriceology Enterprises)
ISBN-10: 0-9838398-3-2

Book Cover Design: *Ozone Media Group*
Editor: Renee Dabney | *The Write Bud*
Interior Design: Jennifer D. Turner | *OK To Dream*

Printed in the USA
10 9 8 7 6 5 4 3 2

WHITE SPACES
MISSING FACES

Why Women of Color Don't Trust White Women

IF YOU ARE NOT A PART OF

THE SOLUTION, YOU ARE A PART

OF THE PROBLEM.

- ELDRIDGE CLEVER

DEDICATION

My Grandmother In Her 40's   Me In My Early 40's

For Rachel, Dottie and Robbie...

I faintly remember my late grandmother Dottie, or Gran as I affectionately called her, share stories about how her mother, Rachel, my great-grandmother was a slave. A slave. A black woman, a human being, living and working as a slave in the home of the brave and land of the free. America! What a tragic shame! I don't recall the details of my great-grandmother's life as a slave, yet I clearly recall my grandmother saying she remembered being in the fields picking cotton alongside her mother Rachel Warr who passed away in 1948.

When my grandmother shared that story with me, I was a young girl, and it carried no real emotional weight at the time. The only association I remember making was that slavery was a horrible experience for black people, and I knew someone who experienced this American horror personally. My young mind couldn't possibly fathom the magnitude of the atrocity committed against black people, my people, and my family. And, yet, I knew clearly the fire of justice was burning within me then.

Sally Noel, Dottie Hardgraves, the same woman, my Gran who changed her birth name, from Sally to Dottie when she moved up North from Memphis, Tennessee to Sioux City, Iowa, because Sally was a notorious slave name and she hated it. My grandmother, born in 1928 in Wynne, Arkansas, grew up on a farm with 19 siblings in Arlington, TN during a time when sharecropping and hired "help" (one step up from slavery) was the norm. In fact, she was the "help" for some white folks during her younger years, and just the thought of it makes my blood boil. Yet, that was typical life for a black woman with a 3rd grade education in the South.

Robbie Jackson, my mother born in 1956 in Memphis, Tennessee was raised during the time of Jim Crow and grew up in the trenches of the first wave Civil Rights movement. She personally experienced segregation and endured the racist climate where black people were treated as second class citizens, if they were treated as human at all. She resisted *Separate but Equal*, persisted through the turbulence of the emergence of grassroots racial justice activism, and she resiliently raised me to be a strong woman without silencing my black girl magic.

These women. My past and present racial justice warrior women and those I will never know are the broad, powerful and resilient shoulders I proudly stand upon today. They are my muse for this message of truth, freedom, liberation, justice and love. They fought, resisted, and persisted so that I could be free to use my voice for the freedom, justice and liberation of black and brown people.

This book is dedicated to the glorious, wise and tenacious black women of my roots who endured the legal violence of whiteness perpetrated upon them by white women, and, in spite of their circumstances, chose to rise into their resiliency. These brave women withstood the *Weapons of Whiteness* used against them during times when they were expected to be silent and submissive so that I can be loud and disruptive to object the illusion of inclusion to demand justice and liberation for black and brown women today.

I am them, and they are me. Just as you are your mother, grandmother and great-grandmother, and they are you. My people had to deal with your people and fight against the oppression that was forced upon them. And today, I'm dealing with you to resist white feminism and its *Weapons of Whiteness* forged against my black existence. Tomorrow must be dramatically different. It's time to lay down your weapons and refuse to indoctrinate your daughters with the tools of destruction.

Until then…I fight and stand resilient for Rachel, for Dottie and for Robbie. And for Tahsahn (my only child and son) and Tyson (my grandson), I show them the warrior way so they are prepared for their own fight. Because being a black man in America is dangerous, yet they too will choose to rise into their resiliency and keep the revolution moving forward.

I also dedicate this book to my stepfather Andrew Jackson, who passed away in October 2016. He was a man of many words and did not flinch when it came to calling out racism. Rest in power Andrew!

Table of Contents
The Truth

INTRODUCTION

Where ever there are white women, there is racism. Where there is racism, there is toxic white feminism. Toxic white feminism ranges from a subtle dismissive assault to a grandiose racist slap in the face. In every space and place where white women exist, women of color who enter these spaces are sure to experience the racist wrath of *Weapons of Whiteness;* therefore and rightfully so, women of color do NOT trust white women.

Engaging in relationships with white women is a psychological risk for many women of color, and "good" white women are the *most* deceptively dangerous. Women of color have doubtful disdain, cautious optimism and deep skepticism about white women, because for centuries, white women have ignored our plight and exploited our experiences for their own edification, entertainment and evolution.

White women have always been intrigued by our skin tone, curious about our hair and often intimidated by our presence and voice. Their poisonous assumptions, racial stereotypes and implicit biases have determined if we are allowed in *their* white space, how far we climb, and if we climb at all. In white women spaces, white women are the equivalent to what they despise, white male patriarchy. In their own solipsistic oblivion, the very oppressive power white women fight against is raging inside of them. White women fight against white male patriarchy, and women of color fight to resist white toxic feminism.

White women are willful instigators, spectators and perpetrators of our pain. Disingenuous relationships riddled with deception, distrust, doubt and danger has been the nature of our relationships with white women since our first encounter with them. From our earliest memories and throughout our adult years, our value has been examined and analyzed through the proverbial and problematic *White Gaze*; the piercing, skeptical eye of white folks questioning and determining whether people of color are worthy of their time and if they are palatable to their psychological palate.

Yes. All white women are dangerous. Especially in the dominion of their White Spaces. You may be saying, "*No, Catrice, not all white women.*" Yes, ALL white women! Every single one of them (including you) belong to the good ole girl's white supremacy club, have been infected with the dis-ease of racism and indoctrinated with *Weapons of Whiteness*. Weapons you've learned from your mothers, aunts and grandmothers on how to engage with and dominate women of color into submission and oppression. White women have devalued our existence, demoralized our history and continue to sharpen their weapons of violation and oppression.

White women historically and collectively have never been our sisters. There's never been a time in history when white women risked their lives or put resources on the line to stand up for black and brown women. White women have yet to unanimously express overwhelming sadness or anger about the state of black and brown women's lives. White women have yet to fight for justice and the liberation of black and brown women's lives. Instead, we, women of color are reminded of the white woman's intrinsic deficiency of empathy for our pain and plight.

Will there ever be a time when white women unanimously express overwhelming despair and outrage about the state of black and brown women's lives? Will there ever be a time where collectively white women risk their lives and put their resources on the line to stand up for black and brown women? Will white women ever create spaces where they refuse to attack, abuse and oppress women of color? Is it possible? Any of it?

Is it possible for white women to cure themselves from the dis-ease of racism? Will white women finally deal with their toxic white feminism and lay down their Weapons of Whiteness to truly be our sisters? Will there ever be a time when women of color can easily, genuinely and consistently trust white women? I don't know. It hasn't happened for centuries, and I'm not sure it can happen now. I do know that NOW is the time for white women to stop being so damn fragile and afraid and do what's right and this guide will help you decontaminate your white spaces.

Women of color have centuries of legitimate reasons to NOT trust white women: in personal relationships, on the job and online. Racism and White Feminism are paramount to why women of color do NOT attend, participate, thrive or stay in white spaces. White spaces are toxic breeding grounds for racial interpersonal violence under the guise of "feminism" and women's empowerment.

White Spaces Missing Faces boldly objects the illusion of inclusion and exposes the unrepentant truth about the Weapons of Whiteness used by white women to silence, marginalize, violate and oppress women of color. White Spaces Missing Faces unearths the covert roots of racial antipathy between white women and women of color and provides radical solutions for relationship reconciliation, reparation and restoration.

White Spaces Missing Faces teaches you how to lay down your Weapons of Whiteness to stop assaulting women of color while creating, cultivating and sustaining an environment where they stay, thrive and flourish by denouncing your own racism and becoming an anti-racist Accomplice.

White Spaces Missing Faces identifies eight reasons women of color don't trust white women and offers candid commentary on what white women need to do to earn and keep the trust of women of color including solutions for decontaminating white spaces. Diversity is dead and inclusion is an illusion, so let's get real about why women of color don't show interest or thrive in your white spaces.

No, we're not going to celebrate the deceptive dance of diversity.

We're not going to coddle the illusion of inclusion.

We're going to identify the problem, call it out for what it is and deal with it without kid gloves.

Racism.

Racism is the reason women of color don't want to participate in your group, club, company or organization.

Racism is the reason women of color do not flourish and thrive in your space.

Racism is the reason women of color eventually enter the revolving door and never look back.

It's time to examine and decontaminate your space.

Especially the skin you live in. The most important space of all.

The Risk of Befriending the Rose

I don't know if it's possible. - It's certainly not necessary.

But, I can tell you what it feels like.

Slow… Insidious…Antagonizing. - Often times psychologically torturous.

An exhausting emotional death - by a thousand paper cuts.

Tiny yet painful cuts. Sometimes invisible - but hurt like hell.

Why do we continue to attempt to hold the Rose… with thorns?…

When we *know* they will prick us, stick us and cause us to bleed.

We see the beauty in the rose. We want to bring it near us.

Yet we know it hurts us.

Often we admire the Rose from a distance because - we just can't take...

another "accidental or unintentional" prick or poke.

We reach for it, and then quickly draw back because we know "it" was

created to poke, pinch and slice our skin with tiny - yet painful cuts.

We know it will draw blood.

Some of us say screw it and choose to *never* reach for the Rose.

Some of us continue to keep our distance from the Rose.

While others - try to figure out how to hold the Rose - as close as possible

without getting wounded.

I don't know if it's possible. It's certainly not necessary.

The Rose was born with thorns. And to hold it - means risk getting cut.

The Rose.

Often deemed as the most revered and desirable flower.

Doesn't matter what shade the petals are. They all have thorns.

It's unavoidable.

Some people say, "*Leave them damn Roses alone!*"
Often I agree. And I do.
The Rose has a name.
She is a White Woman.
To befriend her… to hold her… is to know - that blood will be drawn.
She was created with thorns.
Thorns of unconscious biased beliefs.
Thorns of implicit racial thoughts.
Thorns of intentional and unintentional psychological attacks.
She cuts with… *Weapons of Whiteness*
Denial, blame, justification, and minimization.
She slices your soul with rationalization and defensiveness.
Microaggressions.
Invalidation.
Racial superiority.
And when you finally have had enough trauma…
She cries.
She runs.
She hides.
She's hurt and offended that you would have the audacity - to point out
and complain about her thorns, all while denying the thorns exist.
She's fragile.
You see them.
You've felt them.
You know they're there.
And if you dare attempt to help her see her thorns. She lashes out.
She cuts and cuts, slices and slices and her thorns speak…
I'm not racist. I have black friends.
I'm not racist. I'm married to a black man.
I'm not racist. My children are half black.
I'm not racist. My neighbors are black.
I'm not racist. My brother's wife is black.
I'm not racist. We have black people in our family.
I'm not racist. I work with black people and love them.
I'm not racist. I don't see color.

I'm not racist. I think people are people. We're all human.

Every thorn cuts.

She draws blood.

She wounds.

And every time you reach for her. Every time you attempt to hold her. You know you will be cut.

It doesn't matter what shade the petals are. She was born with thorns.

And to continue to attempt to hold her.

You agree to death by a thousand paper cuts – because racism is trauma.

You agree to participate in the cycle of violence.

You know… the invisible, imminent cycle of violence that many women find themselves in with abusive partners. The cycle --when the relationship begins in the honeymoon phase. You laugh, you talk, you smile. You do lunch. You engage.

It feels good.

You begin to think you can actually have a relationship with the Rose.

Until the day…

You step out of place.

Until the day… you speak truth.

Until the day… you call out the reality of *your* truth.

Until the day you begin to deeply talk about race, racism and white supremacy.

On this day, in this moment, you move into the next phase of the cycle of violence.

She distances herself.

She's quiet.

She's silent.

She's fragile.

She's hurt.

She's now angry!

She lashes out…

She accuses YOU of being the one with the problem. She accuses you of being the one who is starting trouble. She accuses *you* of being the one who is racist.

Punch.

Slap.

Kick.

Your "friend" just attacked and assaulted you. What the hell just happened?

Emotional abuse at its best.

Sometimes you take it and stay.

Sometimes you know your worth and walk away.

Sometimes you fight back and become overwhelmed with racial battle fatigue.

Most times you leave and never come back. Because you've been here before.

If your relationship is slightly beyond superficial. She'll apologize. She'll say she's sorry. She'll ask for your forgiveness.

But not without… some justification, minimization, rationalization and White Fragility galore!

If you forgive her. You willingly move into the next phase of the cycle of violence.

You walk on egg shells – wondering when, not if, it will happen again.

It usually does. She was born with thorns. She was created to cut.

I don't know if it's possible.

It's certainly not necessary.

But, I can tell you this… to befriend her is to experience…

Slow… Insidious…Antagonizing - emotional death.

Death by a thousand paper cuts.

Tiny yet painful cuts that hurt like hell.

So, what happens now?

There are only three options.

Reach for the colorful tulips and daisies instead.

Leave them damn Roses alone or she chooses to remove her thorns.

Yet, a Rose is not a Rose without her thorns. She will always be a Rose.

8 Reasons Women of Color Don't Trust White Women

"I can't believe what you say, because I see what you do."
— James Baldwin

Chapter One: "Collectively white women don't give a damn about women of color."

Chapter Two: "White women notoriously use *Weapons of Whiteness* to assault women of color."

Chapter Three: "Women of color know your claim of colorblindness is a lie."

Chapter Four: "White women love to silence women of color."

Chapter Five: "All white women are racist."

Chapter Six: "White women's thirst for attention marginalizes women of color."

Chapter Seven: "White Feminism is toxic and lethal."

Chapter Eight: "White women have been colluding with white supremacy for centuries."

Has there ever been a time in history when people of color could deeply trust white people collectively?

Why should we trust you now? Are you expecting us to trust you because you woke up from your unconscious social slumber and now are ready to take action?

Nah! - It doesn't work that way. Expect to be deeply untrustworthy until you PROVE IT EVERY SINGLE DAY.

Has there ever been a time in history when white women collectively put their lives on the line for black and brown women? No. And for this reason, women of color do not trust white women.

"IF WOMEN OF COLOR ARE

MISSING IN YOUR SPACE YOU

HAVE A RACISIM PROBLEM."

#CATRICEOLOGY

CHAPTER ONE
Do You See What We See?

> *"Collectively white women don't give a damn about women of color."*
> — *Catriceology*

I can't even begin to count the times I've walked into a space, a meeting, event or an organization and didn't see a soul who looked like me. Not a single black or brown face. I used to be perplexed and upset by the absence of diversity and inclusion, but today, I know *exactly* why this happens in these "so called" inclusive, progressive spaces. Let's start with the brutal truth. Most companies, organizations, groups and spaces don't deeply care about diversity and inclusion. Yes, go ahead and swallow that truth. Because if they did, they would be doing *something* about it, and there wouldn't be the continued need for "diversity training," and I wouldn't be writing this book. Shouldn't leaders and managers just get it by now? I mean really, it's the twenty-first century and America has never been so "brown." So why are companies, organizations and leaders *still* trying to figure this diversity thing out?

Before I dive deeper into the answers to that question, let's start with some fundamentals to make sure we are on the same page. Diversity is an ambiguous word that includes unlimited defining human characteristics and qualities. When you hear the word diversity, you can conclude it includes race, gender, class, socio-economic status, age, ethnicity and a slew of other categories used to honor the differences among people, and, on the other hand, used to discriminate and oppress people. But it can also (and does) include less obvious characteristics such as personality, learning styles, belief systems, thinking styles, and leadership styles. Nevertheless, diversity is important; however, the word *diversity* is simply *not enough* to create communities and professional spaces where *all* women feel a deep sense of belonging and thrive.

The truth is a large number of women of color in predominately "white" spaces are surviving at best. By surviving, I want you to imagine a woman of color in the middle of the ocean with a life jacket on trying to make her way to the shore of safety while fighting against the thrusting, breathtaking waves. She's exerting a lot of energy trying to stay alive, occasionally going under, but somehow emerging again and again, yet still, gasping for air trying to withstand the detrimental elements of her environment. If your company or space is her ocean, you can see why survival is not enough. And I'd put money on it and bet many women of color feel like they are barely surviving in the workplace and white spaces. How do I know? Because I've been there and done that in every single company I've worked at. I've survived at best, and I've had private conversations with hundreds of women of color in my life time, who often feel the same agony of "*just surviving*" in predominantly "white spaces;" even in spaces where it's predominantly women.

Alright, I'm being a bit dramatic with the ocean analogy, but truthfully, that's how it often feels; a daily emotional battle of fighting to survive. Survival can be defined as *"the state or fact of continuing to live or exist, typically in spite of an accident, ordeal, or difficult circumstances."* Let's break that down. Would *you* like to be in spaces, places, groups, companies or organizations where you just simply *exist*? I don't know about you, but to *just* exist in the world is disempowering, lifeless and unfulfilling. I refuse to settle into and accept mediocrity or second best. Would *you* be excited about entering and engaging in spaces where there are constant or consistent "difficult circumstances?" Spaces and places where there is always some challenge, barrier or obstacle? Those types of spaces and places suck; and they suck the life out of you! And every day they are sucking the life out of women of color all over the world.

Now let's take a look at the meaning of thriving! To thrive means to grow, to develop vigorously, to blossom, flourish and prosper. Yes! Now that's what I'm talking about! We all want to be empowered, to be seen, loved, heard, accepted, honored and respected when we show up in the world no matter the space. And in order to thrive in any space the "environment" must be cultivated and conducive for optimal thrival! That means companies, organizations and leaders must intentionally, strategically, aggressively and consistently remove any and all challenges, barriers and obstacles that prevent women of color from thriving, advancing and being successful. I'll share more about exactly how to accomplish this in Chapter Six.

So, here's another truth to digest. If women of color are absent from *your* space, if there are only a few of them showing up or participating, and or if they come and go, *you have a problem*; a serious problem that can be solved. And if you're the leader of the company, group or organization, the problem and the solution rests on *your* shoulders. So if I walk into your space, place, company or organization and there is no one who looks like me or very few of them, it tells me one thing very clearly; *you don't care enough about diversity and inclusion,* and that is offensive and unacceptable!

As you can see, I'm not going to regurgitate the same ole diversity and inclusion message you may be used to. That message only works on the surface level, and, if you are still trying to *master the art of inclusion* in 2017, clearly you must take a deeper dive into what keeps you from just doing it. Maybe you're wondering why a lack of diversity and inclusion is offensive. If you have this problem in your space or organization, it's offensive because it blatantly tells me and other women of color *"we are not welcome, and we don't matter."* If you have a few faces of color in your space or organization it says *"you may be welcome but you really don't belong here."* If you have a few faces of color within your space or organization and they are not actively engaged, holding leadership positions, staying, advancing and thriving, it says *"we see you, and you're welcome, but we don't truly honor your presence and value."*

So how do you begin to solve *your* problem? The first step in solving the problem is to see the problem and view it through a new objective lens with ferocious honesty and truth. The truth is race *still* matters; it always has and always will. You see, women of color do not get the luxury or have the privilege to just be "a woman." Whether they say it, acknowledge it or even know this truth prevails, *it matters; race matters*. Blah! Blah! Blah! Yes, I know race is really not a thing, and that it's a social construct created as a divisive and oppressive tool to access and sustain power and privilege. You can argue that race doesn't matter if you like, and if you do, know that your lack of diversity and inclusion problem will persist and your denial of this truth only perpetuates the problem.

I'll elaborate on why race matters more in the upcoming chapters, but for now, let's get back to the question I posed in the first paragraph of this chapter; *why are companies, organizations and leaders still trying to figure this diversity thing out*? Leaders, companies and organizations are still mystified about how to master the art of inclusion because they do not want to see race, talk about race, deal with race and or address issues of racism. Colorblindness or refusal to see race, leads to unconsciousness, challenges, conflict and cultivates communities that only foster survival if that. If you truly desire to attract, empower and sustain women of color in your spaces, places, companies and organizations, you're going to have to see what you've been taught not to see; the color of their skin and all that their race and culture brings with them. It's a package deal that cannot be separated.

Let's tell the truth. Companies, leaders and spaces don't have a diversity and inclusion problem, they have a racism problem. White spaces with missing faces are unethical, oppressive, bad for your brand and business and just plain wrong. It's especially wrong for *anyone* claiming to understand and value diversity but not willing or able to walk their talk and cultivate it. In fact, it's hypocrisy! If you truly value diversity and want to create an inclusive community or organization where all women know they belong and thrive, it's time for race to matter to you. There is absolutely no other alternative. We, as women of color, SEE our skin and yours, you see it even though you may say you don't, so why not just deal with the realities and complexities of skin color? You can't create the cake without the recipe. And that's part of the problem. Leaders want diverse and inclusive environments but don't have the right recipe or the know how to create the final outcome.

At some point, you have to stop saying "*we're not a very diverse company or organization, we don't know how to create diversity, we don't know how to find women of color, and or we attract women of color but they don't stay.*" All of these statements are tired excuses and are simply unacceptable. Would it be okay for men to say to you that, "*we just don't have many women in our company, we don't know how to find women, and or we don't know how to attract and keep women in our company?*" Hell No! Absolutely not; this would be grossly unacceptable and insulting to you, and you'd be furious if a man said this to you. Am I right? Well, women of color are honestly damn tired of white women not knowing (or choosing not to learn) *how* to figure it out, and many of us are furious that you haven't. I'd suggest you stop making those ridiculous statements because, if we don't give you the "*that's some B.S. side eye look*" directly, we're certainly doing it internally.

It's time for you to see what we see, and then consistently do something about it. *Inclusion is a verb*! Diversity is not enough. I've grown tired of the word diversity. I think it has been squeezed for all its worth. I actually prefer that leaders and managers strive to *become* socially conscious and socially proficient. Notice the difference here. I'm not suggesting that you DO diversity; I'm declaring that you BECOME socially conscious and socially proficient. Doing and creating diversity is superficial. Becoming socially conscious requires personal effort beyond the 9-to-5. It's a deliberate daily choice. It's a lifestyle. It's a new way of thinking, believing and behaving in the world and you do it intentionally 24/7 – 365. More so, it's who you BECOME not what you do.

Becoming socially conscious and socially proficient gives you a new, awakened, and objective lens that allows you to cultivate and sustain anti-racist, inclusive communities and environments. I know exactly why many people don't want to see, talk about or deal with race issues. Because when you see race, that means you *must* also see the ugly dis-ease of racism and how it has benefited some (more often white people) while oppressing others. When you see race, you must acknowledge and own *your own* implicit and explicit biases, prejudices and privileges that keep racism alive and thriving. When you see race and all of the oppressive implications and complications of racism and become conscious of how racism has adversely affected the lives of people, you can't un-see it. You begin to clearly see all of the racial injustices happening in the world. So, the first step in creating inclusive environments where all women know and feel they belong and thrive is to SEE race because it matters. It always will.

Race matters just like gender matters. Imagine if men said, "*Well, I really don't see gender; I just SEE you as a human being.*" Would you believe it? Or would you say, "*Yeah right, you know you see a woman standing before your eyes?*" Of course, you would. It's not acceptable for men to deny they see gender, and then say they are working to create an environment that is gender friendly, gender equal or gender free. Women are *still* fighting for equality and advancement in predominantly male spaces and rightfully so. There's *no difference* between this scenario and when white women make similar statements regarding being color blind and seeing women of color as human beings; different scenario, same harm, oppression and hypocrisy!

It is absolutely critical for you to SEE women of color as women who are of a different race with a different set of challenges, barriers and obstacles to overcome. And to refuse to SEE what we see is a *disconnection, disservice, and it's disempowering.* Yes, of course, you're going to encounter women of color who may think very differently from me. You'll find women of color who may not agree with my perspective. You may even speak to women of color who don't want you to SEE the color of their skin or be concerned with their race. That is going to happen because I do not speak for *every* woman of color in the world, and each woman depending on her race, ethnicity and culture will have unique views and perspectives of her own. However, there's enough research and literature available to support my perspective, and if you're truly invested in inclusion, *your* educational journey will extend beyond this book and my perspective.

"Until the disconnect between value and action is addressed, there will continue to be negative implications for attracting and retaining diverse employees across the nonprofit sector" said Level Playing Field Institute Executive Director Robert Schwartz, Ed.D. "Diversity commitments must move beyond a tagline on a website, and must be followed by specific and strategic actions implemented in order to ensure that diversity becomes a reality within organizations."

If there are missing faces in your predominantly "white spaces" what are *you* going to do about it? Seeing race, talking about race, leaning in to race discussions is the first and most effective step you can take. It is the BIG elephant in the room people pretend they don't see, but they know it's there, and IT isn't going anywhere unless you deal with it. Here's an excerpt from my book *Antagonists, Advocates and Allies* that perfectly illustrates what I have said thus far. I highly suggest you get a copy of the book if you're really ready to do your own personal work to become an Ally and Accomplice for black women, women of color.

Antagonists, Advocates and Allies: Chapter 4

"Let me show you how seemingly small but powerful White Privilege is. After doing an informal assessment of the organization to include staffing patterns, training materials, policies and procedures, shelter rules and the overall guidelines for being accepted into the shelter, I came to this quick conclusion. The organization wanted to reach out to women of color and serve them, yet the staff was ninety-seven percent White; they offered little to no training on how domestic violence is different for women of color for the staff and crisis advocates, the policies and procedures were not culturally sensitive, the shelter rules were created by and for White women, and the overall guidelines for being in the program weren't always conducive for women of color. *Why in the hell would women of color come there, feel wanted, safe and secure and or stay there?* I knew if much of the above did not change that we would be setting women of color up to be re-victimized; thus they would return to their abusers.

There was no ethnic food in the refrigerator. There were no women of color on the artwork on the walls. There was no diversity in the selection of dolls for the little brown girls. There were no hair care products especially for Black women. Many of the materials were not translated into Spanish. Okay, I'm going to stop there, although, I could share other unconscious, privileged observations and truths with you. If a woman of color were to arrive in the shelter, she'd likely be greeted by a White woman who did not understand her culture. A White woman who more than likely could not speak her first language. She'd go upstairs to a refrigerator and pantry full of food that was not a main part of her diet. Her daughters wouldn't have dollies that looked like them. Black women would not even be able to care for their unique hair because there are no ethnic products available. She'd walk around seeing White women running the show and plastered all over the walls. What is the direct and indirect message she would get? "I AM NOT WANTED HERE." And no matter what the staff said, the writing is on the wall.

These women would NOT stay, and many of them didn't for these **seemingly small yet powerful acts of White Privilege**. I knew I

had my work cut out for me, and, because my soul won't let me be silent or passively sit back and watch social and racial injustices occur, I rolled up my sleeves and went to work!

Significant and meaningful internal transformation happened during my two-year tenure there. I was eventually promoted to the Community Education Coordinator and Advocacy Trainer, which gave me the opportunity to make sure the staff and advocates got the diversity and cultural sensitivity training they needed and to be the voice out in the community, making sure OUR women got the services *they* needed with dignity and respect. This was a very fulfilling role and opportunity for me. It was *this* experience that set me on the path to becoming an advocate for women, a social and racial justice activist, a licensed and professional therapist and the visionary of my own empowerment movement for women. **There were so many times I was physically exhausted and emotionally drained for standing up for truth, racism and justice for all, and many times, I wanted to quit, but my soul said otherwise.** I was spiritually tired. I was fatigued. I experienced yet again, *Racial Battle Fatigue*. Ironically, from a group of predominantly White women who had signed on to "empower" ALL women but had either no clue or no interest in how to make sure ALL included women of color, Black women. How can this be? When White women, you, say they empower ALL women, *do they really mean it*? Do you truly know what that entails, and are you *sincerely* and *selflessly* willing to do what it takes to walk your talk? Are you equipped to *truly* empower ALL women, to step outside of your comfort zone and walk your talk? **If not, you're telling a lie**. And trust me, WE know it. Maybe you care and maybe you don't. **If you care, it's time to step up and become an Ally!** If you don't, it's *your* choice to continue to be an Antagonist who harms or an Advocate who is fickle, unreliable and too selfish to *relentlessly* stand in the gap for ALL women."

We see it. We know it. It's undeniable! We, women of color, notice when we are the *only* one or one of few. We see the lack of diversity. We're aware of the lack of inclusion. We not only see it; *we feel it*. And it feels exactly like the predominantly male spaces where men pretend they see you there, yet do very little to show and prove they want you there. It feels like those male spaces where men tell offensive jokes about women with little regard to how you feel. It feels like those male organizations where most of the leaders and managers are men. It feels like those male driven companies where the rules were made by men without taking women into consideration. Yep! The same way being in predominantly male spaces sucks for you; it sucks equally if not more, when women of color are in spaces that predominately consist of white females.

Women of color may come into your space or organization, yet many of them will not stay for all the reasons I've outlined or another. It's time for you to *see what we see* and immediately do something dramatically different to change the landscape of your space and cultivate an environment where women of color belong, engage, advance and thrive. If you're not willing to see race and see what we see, you're not willing to solve your problem and you conspire to keep racism and oppression alive in your space.

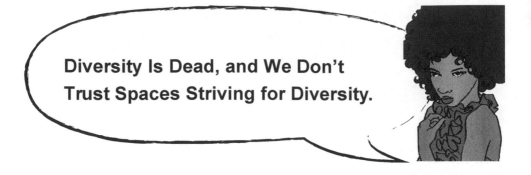

Diversity Is Dead, and We Don't Trust Spaces Striving for Diversity.

If your goal is to diversify your space, you are setting women of color and yourself up for failure and creating a dangerous illusion of inclusion.

WOMEN OF COLOR DO NOT TRUST LIP SERVICE

What is the motive behind your desire of recruitment and representation of women of color?

Do you have a well thought out and effective Inclusivity strategy, Anti-racism plan, and retention plan?

Is your goal tokenism, and do you realize the impact of such dehumanization?

Are you prepared to deal with the alienation and demoralization that women of color feel in predominantly white spaces?

Are you willing to and prepared to continuously and explicitly talk about race and racism within your organization or space?

If you lead or manage a group, club, organization, company, space or place and women of color are being racially oppressed, assaulted, silenced, attacked or marginalized you are responsible and what are you going to do about it?

"WHITE FRAGILITY ISN'T FRAGILE,

IT'S VIOLENT."

#CATRICEOLOGY

CHAPTER TWO

The Struggle Is Not the Same

> *"White women notoriously use weapons of whiteness to assault women of color."*
> — *Catriceology*

So why does it suck *more* for women of color to be the only one or one of few in predominantly white female spaces? We're all women in those spaces so how can that be? Because the struggle is not the same. In fact, it's dramatically different, like night and day. What I am about to share is where white women struggle to get it. This is the moment that you'll likely experience denial, confusion, anger and most likely experience a moment of White Fragility. I'll share a little bit about what White Fragility is, but here's more homework for you. If you want to shift from "*doing diversity on the job*" to becoming socially conscious 24/7, understanding White Fragility is required personal work.

"Fellow White Feminist, it's time for us to take a damn seat and listen." -- Shelby Knox, Feminist Organizer & Revolutionary

I love this quote by Shelby Knox, and *this* is where you must buckle up. This is where you must do *more* than listen; you've got to *hear* what I'm about to say. It is White Fragility more often than not that keeps you from talking about race and actively engaging in race talks. Black and brown women are well versed in this discussion because we talk about race when you don't. We've been talking about it and will continue talking because race matters. And truth be told, White folks are talking about race behind the scenes too. The problem is we are NOT talking to each other about it, and, when we do, it's likely to become a heated discussion. What's also extremely likely is many white women will experience White Fragility during the engagement which usually results in the conversation going nowhere.

White Fragility, term coined and a theory shared by Robin DiAngelo. Robin is a white racism activist who has done extensive research, teaching and consulting on racism and White Privilege. Through her research, and her own personal journey of discovering her own Whiteness, she explored what it meant to be white and wrote a book about it titled "*What It Means to Be White*" and it talks about how white people deny, shift focus and avoid the topic of racism thus resulting in White Illiteracy and White Fragility. Check it out. It will serve as a great resource for you!

Now, let me tell you what White Fragility looks and feels like in real life. Nine times out of ten, if I engage with a white woman about race and racism, I'm likely to hear the following statements from her: "*I don't see color. I'm not racist. I was raised to treat everyone the same. My parents were good white people. We didn't own slaves. I don't believe I have White Privilege. My best friend is black. I grew up with people of color. My sister is married to a black man. But what about reverse racism? I know black people and love them… and so on.*" I could fill the rest of this chapter with all the things I've heard from white women and still have more to write. The above eleven statements are perfect examples of when Robin DiAngelo talks about white folks denying and shifting blame as a tool of White Fragility.

What usually happens next is most white women become defensive, angry, and frustrated which often leads to them crying, and or emotionally checking out or physically walking away from the discussion. White women become mentally, emotionally and physically distressed, overwhelmed and *fragile* during talks about race and racism. Instead of white women leaning in to the uncomfortableness of the conversation, they often can't emotionally handle it and choose to escape, lash out or withdraw in one form or another. Of course, this behavior does not occur with ALL white women, and that's usually with white women who are doing their own *personal racial consciousness* work and or those who are striving to become Allies and Accomplices. It's a rare occasion to engage with white women who do not become overwhelmed during discussions about race.

This is one major reason why you may not want to SEE race let alone talk about it and especially with women of color, because race talks are hard but necessary. I realize you can't (or shouldn't) talk about "race" on the job or within an organization because of potential legal ramifications; however, in your personal life, talking about race and systemic racism is critically necessary. Why? Because quite often, women of color are experiencing some form of racism in their personal or professional life as reported by Sanchez & Davis in their 2010 research article titled "*Women and Women of Color in Leadership. Complexity, Identity, and Intersectionality.*" I'll talk a little more about this in upcoming chapters. I also list it as a suggested resource at the end of the book. It's a worthwhile read.

The 2017 *Women's March on Washington,* while hailed one of the biggest women's marches in American history, horribly struggled and failed to emphasize and amplify the voices and issues faced by women of color and other marginalized women. As a result, this "historic" event soon faced quite a bit of critique and backlash deeming it the "*white women's march on Washington*" and rightfully so. Many black and brown women and their issues were silenced and disregarded in the shadow of motives and platforms such as "smash the patriarchy, equal pay and pink pussy hats [protestors knitted pink hats resembling pussycat ears to wear to defy Donald Trump during the march]." Racial equality and racial justice were not at the forefront of collective marches across the country. Racism was once again forced to the back and not given the urgency it deserves.

White women with their myopic view of feminism stood at the helm of the one-sided movement of equality without compassion or consideration for women of color's need and demand for racial justice. It's painfully obvious that many white women often do not have the desire, skill, emotional bandwidth or resiliency to talk about racism and or to make it a daily priority. Our struggles are *not* the same as pointed out in this passage from a 2010 article in *American Psychologist* referenced earlier.

> "*The situation facing women of color is more complex than that faced by White women. Chief among the causes of additional complexity is the manner in which sexism has been emphasized without consideration of other forms of discrimination. White females, who share the same skin color as most male leaders, can more easily focus exclusively on gender discrimination and may overlook the influence of race and ethnicity on perceptions of leadership (Suyemoto & Ballou, 2007). Women of color can also face "gendered racism" when they are unable to separate the individual effects of each aspect of their identities (Blake, 1999). A woman who feels that she is experiencing discrimination must decide if this prejudice is due to race, ethnicity, gender, or some other dimension of her identity.*"

The struggle is not the same! If you are convinced that all women suffer from the *same* discrimination and oppression, this is a significant barrier to truly understanding the complexities and challenges unique to women of color. Now this is where you need to really hear what I'm about to say. If women of color who work in or are a part of a "woman's" organization, company or group that's comprised of all women, and experiences racism, who then is her oppressor? Who is offending her? Who is to be held accountable for the racism she is experiencing within your environment? THAT is the question to be honestly answered.

Collectively, women (most times white women) are quick to speak about and against the oppressive nature of Toxic Masculinity, which can be defined as the many ways in which patriarchy is harmful and refers to the socially-constructed attitudes and behaviors that describe the "masculine" gender as violent, unemotional, and sexually aggressive. In other words, the ways in which men and masculinity continuously violate, oppress and victimize women (and unknowingly themselves). It is Toxic Masculinity that spawned and propels the women's movement and "feminism" as we know it today. Women all over the world are being negatively affected by patriarchy and Toxic Masculinity. This is why we created "women only" spaces, places, clubs, groups and organizations, to create a safe, supportive and oppression free environment for women to thrive.

But all women are *not* thriving in these "women only" spaces, particularly and pervasively women of color. In creating such spaces, women have for the most part removed or excluded men, yet there is an invisible yet undeniable toxicity that still persists. I like to compare this invisible tranquilizer to the potency of carbon monoxide. Women of color *know* it permeates and lingers in the air of these "women only" spaces even though its presence can't be seen. Women of color *know* if they remain in spaces, where this invisible toxicity prevails, they will eventually endure a slow and painful emotional and spiritual death.

THIS is ONE of the reasons women of color don't come or don't stay in your "places." Let's give that reason a name and make it clear. Women of color often don't come into your organization, group or space because the invisible yet lethal toxicity that permeates your space is called White Feminism. White Feminism is the equivalent to Male Toxicity. White Feminism generally ignores Intersectionality, the important yet often ignored intersection between race and gender (among many other identity characteristics). I'll share more on Intersectionality later but for now let this sink in; *White Feminism is the equivalent to Male Toxicity.* The same way that men consciously and unconsciously oppress women is the same way White women consciously and unconsciously oppress women of color.

If you're feeling irritated, upset or emotionally charged right now by phrases like White Fragility and White Feminism, this is where you take Shelby Knox's advice and *"take a damn seat and listen."* This is not the time to shut down or turn away. This is the time to go beyond leaning in and instead leap into your ability to talk about race, racism and why your organization, group, or space is a revolving door for women of color. This is the moment you sprint to the revolving door and disconnect the automatic revolve button. If you don't do this, please don't say you want to bring women of color into your spaces and places. Keep listening and hearing this message.

Yes! It sucks more for women of color to be in White Feminist spaces because there is the illusion of inclusion dripping in feminist theory that perpetuates the façade that we are welcome. It sucks because white women and women of color both know the pain patriarchy creates in our lives, and we attempt to unite at this intersection of gender. Yet we will never be united until White Feminism is dismantled and true feminism that believes in, embodies and actively pursues the elimination of racism becomes the unshakable foundation of feminism.

Feminism will not activate its full power until white women understand that Intersectionality is real and relevant and that race always matters. When you actively seek out, invite in and encourage women of color to participate in your space, you are also inviting in all the positive and "negative" aspects of what it means to live in black or brown skin. It's a package deal that cannot and should not be separated. So don't invite us in if you refuse to hear about and address the unique challenges and barriers we face that are often put in place by you, white women. That would be hypocrisy and hypocrisy is intentional oppression.

If you want to create, cultivate and sustain environments where women of color thrive, you must embody an intersectional perspective and an anti-racist way of being for optimal success. Let's talk about this potentially dangerous intersection called Intersectionality. If you imagine a busy intersection on any given street, you know the potential for fatality. Each car and driver on the street is focused on getting where *they* need to go and are often selfishly doing so. Some drivers are cautious at the intersection, some are reckless and others are very careful to know the intersectional rules and courtesies and abide by them. Nevertheless, there is always potential danger and detriment (sometimes fatalities) at the intersection.

If you put five different women in a room to talk about how patriarchy is painful, they are going to experience insult at the intersection. They are going to experience oppression at the intersection; women will be misunderstood, ignored and possibly blamed in the process. These women bring a multitude of characteristics, behaviors, thoughts and experiences into the circle of conversation, and there is sure to be conflicting views and experiences. There's no avoiding the clash and crash when differences collide.

Now let's change the dynamics of this conversation circle. What if four of the five women participating in this discussion are white and the fifth woman is black or Native American? There will still be clash and crash by default; however, the woman of color is going to have a dramatically different experience about how painful patriarchy has been to her. She not only will express any current patriarchal offenses, but she also consciously and unconsciously brings with her a legacy of centuries of very specific patriarchy; white male patriarchy that has oppressed her and her people for decades. And when she boldly calls it out and clearly distinguishes this "race" difference, white women in the circle (unless they've done a lot of personal racial justice work) will take offense and quickly begin to defend the oppression.

The defense shows up like this; they will shift the focus and refuse to talk about it, minimize the frequency and duration of the oppression, rationalize why the offense occurred or why it's no longer happening, justify the behavior by saying it happened so long ago, and or they will flat out deny that it still happens. Two very critical things happen when this occurs. First, the woman of color has been re-victimized by her female friends or colleagues through their justification, minimization, rationalization and denial. Second, the woman of color feels unheard, invalidated and unvalued and quickly concludes *"these are not my sisters; these are women pretending to be my sisters."*

What's even more important to understand in this situation is the woman of color knows what just happened to her and quite often the white women would never see themselves as her oppressor. The white women will more than likely view the conflict as a personality conflict whereas the woman of color knows it was undeniably a racial conflict. There may never be true understanding or agreement on what happened; but one thing is for sure, the woman of color knows it's not safe to share her true experience in this white space and thus learns how to *survive* the environment while sacrificing her true value and power. Every single time the woman of color is in this type of situation; she remembers what happened and may choose to just be seen and not heard. And every time she does this a piece of her soul dies. She remains silent to survive, while white women continue on the journey of thrival without taking responsibility for their oppression.

INTERSECTIONALITY

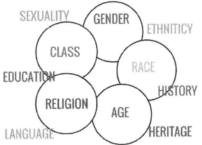

"overlapping or intersecting social identities and related systems of oppression, domination, or discrimination."

If you're going to intentionally invite women of color into your spaces and places, you had better truly understand Intersectionality and its possibility to create pain or progress in the lives of women of color. You can remain unconscious or you can wake up to the importance of Intersectionality and use it to create progress within your organization or space as a primary tool for creating inclusive, thriving environments. There's no such thing as an *oppression free* women's space. The struggle is not the same. And if by chance the woman of color in the scenario is lesbian, an immigrant, is poor and doesn't speak English well, the likelihood of re-victimization, offense and oppression triples and intensifies.

White spaces for women of color are dangerous places, but they don't have to be. If you manage or lead a space for women, it's your responsibility to make it as safe as possible. In your quest to become inclusive, it's highly important that you also know and respect that women of color are NOT your teachers. It is 100% YOUR responsibility to become educated about the complexities of living while black and brown and to understand the unique challenges women of color consistently face. It is NEVER okay to ask them to teach you. To do so is oppressive and a form of racism; just don't do it! Want to know why? A simple Google search will get you started. Educate yourself!

Creating inclusive environments where women of color thrive will require you to get uncomfortable, to *leap* in, and to refuse to become fragile, to educate yourself and do your own work to become socially conscious and socially proficient. It will require you over your lifetime to continue to take several seats and listen and hear what women of color have to say without minimizing it, justifying, rationalizing, shifting the focus or blaming them for their experiences. The struggle is NOT the same. You must believe, accept, honor and respect this truth. I caution you to NOT request unity and solidarity from black and brown women if you're not willing to engage in raw conversations about racism. Especially since YOU are their oppressor! Are you ready to admit to and own up to how you have racially oppressed women of color?

"Women are not a monolithic group. Black and white women contend with very different workplace challenges. Initiatives that effectively identify and retain top talent must consider the unique challenges black women face and the leadership aspirations they offer." – Valerie Purdie-Vaughns [Professor of Psychology at *Columbia University and Columbia Business School.*]

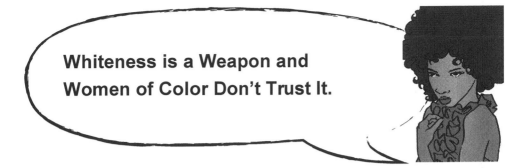

Whiteness is a Weapon and Women of Color Don't Trust It.

Yes, I know you did not choose to be born with white skin, and women of color did not choose to be born with black or brown skin. So, let's just get over that and deal with the reality of the power, privilege and pain associated with skin color. *You may not see color, but women of color always see your whiteness and know what it can do. Women of color know how dangerous your whiteness is.*

WOMEN OF COLOR HAVE CENTURIES OF REASONS TO NOT TRUST WHITENESS

In what ways have you used your whiteness as a weapon? Have you used any of these toxic tactics when engaging with women of color in person and or online?

White Entitlement: The conscious and unconscious belief and or expectation that people of color should talk nicely to you about racism, they should watch their tone and not become angry, they should not call you out in public and or in front of other people, and or they should teach or educate you and be patient with you while you learn. White entitlement also shows up when you think you know more about racism than people of color. Do you believe you know what's best for people of color?

White Innocence: Insistence on not having any responsibility in personal or collective acts of racism or racial violence against people of color and or being guilty of passively preserving and perpetuating racism by being silent and complicit. White innocence shows up when you passionately deny knowing when you've acted in racist ways and is also known as White Ignorance.

White Silence: Knowing white supremacy exists, that you benefit from white privilege and seeing acts of racism occur around you, yet choosing to stay silent. Choosing to stay comfortable, refusing to call people out on their racism, remaining complacent and refusing to use your white privilege to disrupt and dismantle racism and white supremacy.

White Fragility: An emotional state in which the slightest amount of racial stress triggers defense mechanisms (denial, minimization, rationalization, justification, derailment, avoidance, projection, deflection and intellectualizing) and feelings of irritability, anger, frustration, guilt, shame, and fear thus causing you to argue, cry, run away, become silent and or shut down. This especially occurs during discussions about racism with people of color and when you are called out on your racism.

How to Use Your Weapons for Good:

- Identify and own your racist weapons so you can lay them down for once and for all.

- Get uncomfortable and do not allow the toxic status quo of whiteness in your space to rule.

- Speak up because silence perpetuates racism; call out racism when you see it.

- Racism is everywhere. Look for it (especially within yourself) and dismantle it.

- Move to the side and let voices of color be at the center and in front.

- Specifically acknowledge Anti-Blackness racism, its pervasiveness and get involved in the *Black Lives Matter* movement.

- Emotionally and financially support black and brown women. Showcase them, hire them, promote them, collaborate with them, buy from them, refer them, and partner with them.

"WOMEN OF COLOR DON'T

BELIEVE YOU WHEN YOU SAY

YOU ARE COLORBLIND."

#CATRICEOLOGY

CHAPTER THREE

You Can't See Because of Colorblindness

> *"Women of color know your claim of colorblindness is a lie."*
> — *Catriceology*

If you've been taught that being colorblind is a good thing, it's time to *unlearn everything you know* about this untruth. The first step in the unlearning is to stop saying "*I don't see color and or I treat everyone the same.*" First because it's a lie. You DO see color, because it's impossible not to, and second, you don't treat everyone the same as that is impossible as well. Colorblindness and every aspect of it is counter-intuitive to creating inclusive communities. To deny or refuse to see the beauty of a woman of color's skin is to minimize the challenges she faces as a result of living in her black or brown skin.

Living and engaging with a colorblind approach means you willingly refuse to SEE and acknowledge the personal, social, and historical perspectives and experiences of women of color. That makes absolutely no sense at all, and did you know that colorblindness is a form of racism? Colorblindness does NOT foster racial harmony; it perpetuates racial divide and willful ignorance of your own implicit and explicit biases. Colorblindness allows you to stay in your comfort zone and not examine how your privilege and power oppresses the very women you want to include. *Colorblindness is for cowards who don't want to talk about racism.*

Look at it this way. You may think you want men to NOT see your gender or to see you as a *woman*, but that's not very effective if you truly want to succeed, prosper and thrive in male dominated spaces. No doubt, women experience challenges in the world that men generally do not. Do you *really* want men to see you and treat you like "just one of the guys?" Or would you prefer men to see you as a competent, valuable, worthy and qualified woman who happens to be in a predominantly male space? You should NOT have to show up, act like or pretend to be a man to succeed, prosper and thrive in a predominantly male space. That's the way it should be. So what does this have to do with you as a white female leader?

When men refuse to examine how their male privilege has afforded them opportunities and or caused them to oppress women, they won't be able to mindfully and intentionally NOT oppress them. The same is true for you. As a white woman, you have been afforded opportunities and privileges women of color have not. As a result of this white privilege, you have power that women of color do NOT. If your power and privilege goes unacknowledged and unchecked, *you too* will offend and oppress women of color intentionally or unintentionally. You cannot and should not expect women of color to just be treated like "one of the girls."

They are NOT just "one of the girls." Women of color *know* they cannot show up like white women do, do certain things white women do and or be perceived as white women are, even by white women. The same way you do not want to be treated like just "one of the guys," women of color do not want to be treated like "one of the girls." Most women of color know that in order to survive in predominantly white spaces, they must *shift*. And this shifting is a conscious and unconscious (conditioned) response to potentially dangerous stimuli, kind of like the automatic response of fight and flight in the face of danger.

During a research project conducted by Charisse Jones and Kumea Shorter-Goodman, Ph.D., called the *African-American Women's Voices Project*, they discovered a phenomenon that African-American women tend to *shift* (alter their behavior = aka lead a double life) when in predominantly white environments, situations and generally just moving through the world. The project included in-depth interviews and surveys with 333 African-American women all over the United States between the ages of 18-88. These were women of different backgrounds to include income, marital status, sexual orientation, and educational backgrounds. Essentially, they were asked "how they deal with experiences of racial and gender discrimination in their lives and what helps them to deal or cope with the discrimination."

The women reported that 97 percent of the time they were very much aware of the negative stereotypes African-American women face daily, and 80 percent of the time they were adversely and personally affected by the persistent sexist and racist assumptions. And in order to cope with or deal with the racist and sexist oppression, they've learned how to *shift* to survive. This is not *new* information; it just proves African-American women have *always* had to learn how to *survive* in a white and patriarchal society. The shifting is real, and it is happening still today in predominantly white spaces. I know. I've had to *shift* and *shift* and still in 2017; society requires that we, women of color, *shift* to survive.

So, what does shifting look and feel like? Shifting happens when a black woman goes in for an interview and knows she *must* speak "proper" English while arresting any cultural dialects, words or phrases to be considered for the job. Many black women speak differently at work than they do in private and or with other black people. While working in predominantly white spaces, black women tend to mute their natural expressions, minimize hand or body gestures and or selectively choose their words to "fit in" or survive. Of course, this is not the case for ALL black women and women of color, but this shift has been happening since chattel slavery.

Black women had to quickly learn *how* to talk to Massa and Missy (The Masters white wife = aka white women), *what* to say and what not to say and when not to speak otherwise they'd suffer horrific consequences, even death. When they returned to their slave quarters their tone, language and expressions were quite different, representative of their authentic self. These black women learned how to survive in the white patriarchal society because their life *depended* on it. Once free and during the Jim Crow era, shifting continued; black women still *had to* stay in their place, bite their tongue and depress any sense of independence or confidence or they'd be subject to legal and illegal punishment.

The history is there for your reading and understanding. Educate yourself! If you examine how black women in particular have been forced (directly or as a means of survival) to minimize their existence, silence their voice, say yes when they want to say no, shrink to subdue, watch their tone and be seen and not heard. *All* of it done for survival. Because of the stereotypes, discrimination and racism that black women have and still face, many of them consciously and unconsciously sacrifice themselves to be accepted, included, promoted and advanced. Every day they internally and externally fight to prove they are not "those" stereotypes. They shift.

According to Jones and Shorter-Gooden's book, *Shifting: The Double Lives of Black Women in America*, shifting looks like this: *"Shifting is often internal, invisible. It's the chipping away at her sense of self, at her feelings of wholeness and centeredness – often a consequence of living amidst racial and gender bias. To shift is to work overtime when you are exhausted to prove that you are not lazy. It's the art of learning how to ignore a comment you believe is racist or to address it in such a way that the person who said it doesn't label you as threatening or aggressive. It's over preparing for an honors class to prove you are capable, intelligent and hard-working. It's feeling embarrassed by another African-American who seems to lend a stereotype truth, and then feeling ashamed that you are ashamed. And sometimes shifting is fighting back."*

Shifting is so tiring, overwhelming and fundamentally unnecessary. Why can't women of color just show up and be without worrying about the societal rules of how they are *supposed* to show up and be? You see… women of color cannot always just show up and be *"one of the girls;"* so stop asking and expecting them to! I've worked at two women's organizations in my lifetime, and both of them oozed with toxic femininity. Both organizations had missions designed to empower women and they were some of the most disempowering and toxic places I've ever worked, women cat-fighting with each other, childish clique after clique and the fakery of women calling themselves *colorblind* when I know damned well they SAW my beautiful brown skin every day.

I never felt like *"one of the girls."* Whenever I spoke up about concerns in the workplace with an assertive voice, I was deemed angry (stereotype). When I called out REAL injustices, I was seen as "stirring the pot or race-baiting (stereotype)." When I was naturally and boldly expressive, I was seen as too animated or dramatic (stereotype). When I disagreed, I was seen as combative (stereotype). I wasn't doing anything but being a confident woman in my skin, and that is threatening (stereotype) in predominantly white spaces, even when those spaces are filled with predominantly white women who should be more understanding of how oppressing it is to live under the thumb of the powers that be. But nah! It's the same. White women oppress women of color all the time, even in so called "safe spaces."

There has not been ONE job in my lifetime that simply allowed or encouraged me to just be me. I've never worked in an environment where I could just be a beautiful black woman with obvious brown skin and not be seen as aggressive, overbearing, outspoken or threatening in some kind of way. There were always conditions: spoken and unspoken. In every predominantly white space, I too had to shift to survive until one day, I decided I deserved more and better than the anguish of wearing a façade simply to exist. In 2008, I finally took off my mask and cape to start my own business so I could be free to be me. White feminist toxicity is lethal! White women are dangerous and they always use their weapons against women of color.

If you truly desire to create, cultivate and sustain communities, spaces and organizations that welcome, support and empower women of color, you MUST stop saying you are colorblind and realize how delusional, damaging and disempowering this is. Sure, women of color don't want you to treat them different because of their race and the color of their skin, but they do want you to see the color of their skin and attempt to understand what positive and negative consequences they face because of the color of their skin. To see their skin is to see, honor, appreciate and value their culture, heritage, traditions, values, beliefs and yes barriers.

You have some unlearning to do. It's time to *unlearn everything you know* about this untruth that colorblindness is a good thing. If you want to shut down the revolving door within your company, organization or group, one of the first actions to take is to SEE who is not in the room or at the table. The next time (and every time after) you go to a meeting, an event, a conference or any gathering, notice who is NOT there. If you don't see large amounts of women (people) of color, there is a problem. There is a racism problem. There is a revolving door set on high speed. If you truly want women of color in your space, it's up to you to get them there. And before you do, make sure the environment is ready to receive, support and empower them; otherwise you will set them up for *survival* and failure. The environment must be anti-racist.

Yes, I know. When you begin to honestly *see* the color of people's skin, it means you'll have to honestly see your own and what that means for women of color. You'll have to see and own up to the power and privileges you have that they don't. You'll have to admit to and confront your own racism. You'll have to see and work to reconcile all the ways that white women (you) have historically and currently oppress women of color. When you see your white skin, you'll have to leap outside of your comfort zone to become an ally and accomplice for women of color who face sexism and racism. You'll have to challenge the racist status quo within your group and organization and call out the racism, discrimination and exclusivity when you see it happening. You'll have to check yourself when you catch yourself being the perpetrator of racism.

Oh yes! You will have to do *all* these things and *more.* You see, it's not enough to see women of color and invite them into your spaces. You must completely evolve from the inside out and reconstruct the spaces in which you want them to come. Trust me when I say, women of color who are *woke* (highly aware of racism and injustice) will know without a doubt whether you've done your own personal anti-racist work and whether your environment is an inclusive space where *she* can thrive. She'll know whether your intentions are pure and authentic or whether you are putting on (hiding your weapons) to get her in.

Refusing to be colorblind, being consistently intentional about how you engage with women of color, and reconstructing the environment of your space will begin to slow down the revolving door, but that is just the beginning. It's not enough to slow down the revolving door; the door must be removed piece by piece, and so the deconstruction continues.

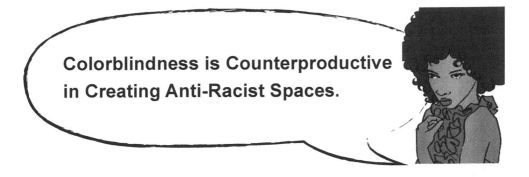

Colorblindness is Counterproductive in Creating Anti-Racist Spaces.

Women of color KNOW your claim of being colorblind is first a lie and second selfish. You don't really believe you don't see color, do you? You don't really believe that women of color *believe* that you don't SEE the color of their skin, do you? It's a lie! Stop saying you're colorblind. Secondly, we also know your claim of color blindness is not to offer acceptance and unity for our sake, yet claiming colorblindness is a cop-out that keeps you comfortable so you don't have to talk about race and racism. Just like we see your whiteness, you see our color. And when you say this to women of color please expect to get the side-eye and to NOT be trusted.

HOW WOMEN OF COLOR TRANSLATE THE DECLARATION OF COLORBLINDNESS

When women of color hear white people say they are colorblind these are common translations of what they really hear you say and what they are thinking.

- *Now you know damn well you see my black or brown skin.*
- *You're lying. I don't believe you.*
- *Really? I don't trust you.*
- *Nice. Let's see how long this lasts.*
- *As soon as I make a mistake or express myself, you'll see color.*

- *If you don't see my skin color, you don't see me.*

- *I better be cautious of this person; they are bound to racially assault me.*

- *She/he is racist. That was offensive.*

- *If you don't see my color, you don't see my pain, challenges and barriers.*

- *I wonder how many other black and brown people you've offended with this statement.*

- *She/he doesn't even know she/he made a racist statement.*

- *I'm definitely going to have to "shift" around this person.*

And finally, if you say this to a person of color, please expect to possibly be confronted and called out on your racist behavior. Being colorblind or engaging from a colorblind perspective is dangerous and detrimental to the emotional wellness of people of color. Instead, it's essential you see the color of their skin and value, honor and respect their beautiful differences to create a space where they do not have to shift and can thrive.

How to Create a Space Where Women of Color Do Not Have to Shift:

- *Don't expect women of color to instantly trust you or be your friend. They have countless legitimate reasons NOT to trust you or feel safe being your friend.*

- *Identify and work on eliminating your own implicit racial biases and stereotypes about women of color and deconstruct them.*

- *Do not treat women of color as tokens, ask them to speak for or represent their entire race and or expect them to willingly engage in your space prematurely (before they trust you).*

- *DO NOT ask women of color to teach you about racism or their culture. It's offensive, and it's your responsibility to educate yourself.*

- *Do not engage in fetishism of women of color (constantly praising their beauty, strength, courage or other personal characteristics to make them feel super-human or God-like).*

- *Refuse to demonstrate White Fragility behavior; it's violent. Period.*

- *Increasing your social intelligence and strengthening your emotional intelligence muscle will dramatically improve your relationships and engagements with women of color.*

- *Lead with integrity by offering opportunities for your members/staff to learn about racism, white supremacy and oppression and how to dismantle it personally and socially.*

- *Get comfortable with the various expressions of women of color and how they choose to naturally show up without censoring or tone policing their voice.*

- *Just allow women of color to be who they naturally are without questioning their intelligence and expecting them to act and show up how you want them to (like white people).*

"WHERE THERE ARE

WHITE WOMEN, THERE IS

RACISM."

#CATRICEOLOGY

CHAPTER FOUR

The Truth Hurts

> *"White women love to silence women of color."*
> — *Catriceology*

"*The truth will set you free, but it will first piss you off,*" A quote by Gloria Steinem that is very true. I'm sure you never imagined part of the reason women of color continue to access the revolving door of your company, space or organization is quite possibly because of how YOU show up in those spaces. People leave companies and organizations because of people. This is true as well for women of color in predominantly white spaces. And since this chapter is about truth, the truth is quite often, women of color leave predominantly white spaces because of white people. Whoa! Wait a minute. Hold on.

It isn't white people in general that turns women of color away; it's *white environment culture* that is overbearing and oppressive. You should know where I'm going with this if you've allowed my previous words to sink in; but, just in case you're still struggling, I'll explain more. Better yet, let me paint a picture for you. Imagine you just got hired as manager at a large, well known company where 90 percent of the staff was women of color. You walk in on your first day and there are women from diverse ethnicities and cultures, African-American, Asian, Latina, Native-American, Nigerian, Brazilian, Mexican and just a few that you can count on two hands, are white women.

You search for your boss, and, when you find her, you are greeted by a brown skin woman with a bit of an accent. She's a lovely woman, very friendly, and you believe you and she are going to hit it off well. As you move through the building on your first day, you notice things. You notice different personalities, different body shapes, different ways of doing things and lots of different stuff. And yes, you notice you are one of a few white women, and you're surrounded by amazing women of color, and maybe you don't think too deeply about what that really means at *this* moment.

But eventually, you discover the environment is different than environments you're used to. The nice, *well-intended* women of color are curious about your hair, want to touch it and ask you endless questions about what it's like to have hair like that. You notice when you bring in leftovers from your favorite Irish dish, your co-workers come into the break room saying "*eww what's that smell*?" They ask you ridiculous questions about your choice of cuisine on a regular basis, and it makes you uncomfortable. You notice they talk about topics and subjects you either don't know about and or have no interest in; it's a challenge to relate. You're starting to feel out of place, but you love your job and need it so you tough it out.

As days past, you notice the artwork on the walls of powerful women don't include images of white women. You notice that 97 percent of the client documents and forms are written in foreign languages. You wonder how the few English speaking white clients who do come in for services will understand the forms. This upsets you. You ask "*can the forms be translated into English,*" and your boss gives you the *but why* look. She tells you that not many of the clients are English speaking anyway, so it's not necessary to translate ALL of the forms. You disagree and begin trying to figure out how to get the forms translated.

It's now time for you to start seeing new clients. You begin to notice you get the referrals for the white clients who come in for services. You wonder why and the response you get is *"well, we thought they'd be more comfortable with someone who looks like them."* This infuriates you, but you keep on doing your job because you don't want to make waves. Your clients begin to say things like *"I'm glad you're here because I would not feel comfortable sharing my truth with the other staff, or I was afraid to come in for services because I wasn't sure how I would be treated."* These statements make you wonder what is really going on within this organization.

You decide to bring up your concerns at the next staff meeting. You KNOW you've got to come extra prepared to get your point across and be taken seriously. You're nervous. You wonder how your presentation will be perceived because every other time you've tried to bring up valid points and issues you've been ignored or made to feel like you're just *too* sensitive. You muster up the courage to share your thoughts, and you notice that the other women around the table are either in shock, ignoring what you say and or denying that your feelings and observations are true.

You're exhausted. They didn't hear you. They didn't believe you. They blew you off and encouraged you to not get too "racial." You are livid! You're not crazy. You KNOW these things are happening and that your feelings are real. Days later you notice that your colleagues are not as friendly towards you. They are cordial but that's about it. And to your surprise one of your white colleagues comforts you and says *"I see it too. I've been trying to speak up about it, but they don't want to listen."* You and her begin talking more about the changes that need to be made, and it feels good to know that someone else sees what you see and believes what you believe. It's this ONE *white* colleague that helps you make through every day of survival on the job.

Working at this organization becomes overwhelming for you. You begin to disassociate. You do your job, stick to yourself and clock out to have *survived* another day. It seems like they don't see you, hear you and or value your contribution. Every day going forward you feel like an outsider. Your colleagues aren't horrible people. They're nice people. They treat you kindly. You love your work. Yet, inside you know *something* isn't right. You know if you stay you will die inside. You know if you stay that you'll survive at best. You know that you will surely not thrive. This space is becoming toxic and your emotional well-being is at risk.

The culture and the environment were not ready to receive you because that's the way it's *always* been, and they "don't know any better." They didn't have the eyes to see life from your perspective. They only could see through the lens of being the dominant group. They aren't bad people. They didn't *intend* to ignore, silence or hurt you, but they did, unintentionally and repeatedly. The truth is that you're dying of a thousand invisible paper cuts. They sting. They throb. They hurt and no one can see or feel them but you. And since this is the case, you are *the one* deemed to have a "problem." YOU are the one making waves, starting trouble, stirring the pot, ruffling feathers and being divisive.

At some point, you begin to wonder whether you are imagining things, whether you are blowing things out of proportion and or whether it really is you that is stirring a pot that only you can see. Yet, deep down in your soul you *know* it's all real, very real although you can't concretely prove it. You are in the middle of some crazy mess and are not sure how to deal with it, solve it or escape it. Every day your work life becomes more miserable while your colleagues seem to be happily going about their business, totally unaffected and unaware of what's happening.

That's it! You've had enough. You just can't take it anymore. It's time for you to push the button on the revolving door. You decide to resign and take your energy elsewhere. Many of your colleagues are shocked and say they are sad to see you go. You feel a sense of relief as you plan to heal your wounds and move on to the next opportunity. You're scared and excited at the same time because you hope the next space will be *different*, yet you know they're usually *always* the same, welcoming but not inclusive. Regardless, you know it's time to go. So you pack up your belongings and enter the revolving door.

What I've just illustrated to you is a frequent, familiar and painful experience for women of color in white spaces, and yes, white female spaces too. And what's more sad is the predominantly white female spaces truly *believe* they are not oppressive because they too experience misogynistic oppression, which is very true. This is a perfect example of the collateral damage that happens at the intersection of race and gender for women. That's why a deep, working understanding of intersectionality is critical especially in women's spaces.

This may be harsh, but it's true. Predominantly white spaces are often filled with an invisible yet lethal set of values, beliefs, expectations and biases, the equivalent to carbon monoxide. And when a woman of color is exposed to such environments, it can be deadly, emotionally, psychologically and spiritually. I know this from personal experience. The scenario I previously described happened to me, and I left out so many other disempowering things that happened to me during that time. In fact, every single place I've worked in the past I have experienced this carbon monoxide like environment. And each time I packed up my things and entered the revolving door.

Remember, I said that it's not enough to acknowledge or slow down the revolving door. You must deconstruct it piece by piece so it doesn't exist. It's a challenge but possible. You can no longer take the risk to going out to recruit women of color into your groups, spaces and organizations without first changing the culture and environment in which you are inviting them into. If you fail to do this, I guarantee you will set them up for failure. I know you do not want women of color to purposely fail right? Of course not, that's why impact is always more powerful than intent. You may not intend to offend or impress, but when you do, the impact is greater than you can imagine. It's psychological and emotional abuse!

At the beginning of this chapter, I said "*People leave companies and organizations because of people. This is true as well for women of color in predominantly white spaces. And since this chapter is about truth, the truth is quite often, women of color leave predominantly white spaces because of white people.*" Gulp! It's still true. So what are you going to do with this truth? How will you begin to become an awakened, conscious, anti-racist and inclusive person and ensure that *your* space or environment is *ready* to receive, support, and empower women of color?

Of course you can't do it alone, but you can be the catalyst that changes the culture and climate in the spaces you are a part of. People often speak of change, and many don't become the change. So, if you are ready to be the change, it starts with you. What truth do you need to tell, face and address about your own biased and racist thoughts and feelings about people of color? Don't say you don't have any because we all have biases. And, if you're not honest with yourself, those biases will show up in how you communicate and engage with women of color. Dig deep and tell the *truth* to yourself even if you don't tell it to anyone else. Tell the truth about your racism!

Where do your biased thoughts and beliefs come from? Where or who did you learn them from? Are they *really* true? What "proof" do you have? How are they serving your highest good? Are they creating a bridge between you and women of color or a breakdown? These are powerful questions to meditate on and come up with honest and concrete answers. There's a saying that goes a little something like this, *"what's in the heart eventually rolls off your lips."* In other words, those deep-seated, unconscious beliefs you have about people of color residing in your heart will eventually be exposed in your words given the right opportunity. It happens to the best of us, and it will happen to you. Check your heart. Your biases live there. Your racism lives there!

Maybe by now you're feeling some kind of way about what I've shared. Maybe this is the first time you've heard such things. Maybe you're pissed off. Maybe you're confused or sad. And maybe, just maybe I'm making sense, and it's starting to come together for you. If not, keep reading and staying open to this truth. You and I both know I cannot speak for every black or brown woman, yet I've been in this black body for forty-seven years now and trust me, *I know more about what that's like than you.* And if you ever get the opportunity to genuinely and honestly engage with other black and brown women beyond the surface of superficial conversation, you just might hear an echo of the words I speak. Pay attention you'll hear and see it too.

You have the personal power to do *your* part to ensure that when women of color enter your space they come into an environment that says "*you're wanted here, we need you, we see you, we honor you, we value you and we are committed to doing whatever it takes for you to feel safe, seen, and to prosper and thrive.*" And this is especially true when women of color enter your own personal space, not just the physical environment but when they personally engage with you. Lay down your weapons!

There is no human in the world who knows YOUR personal life experience like you know it. The same is true for her, women of color. You may be educated, savvy and knowledgeable about a lot of things, but you'll *never* know what the life experience is of black and brown women. And besides, this work I'm calling you to do is more about you than it is about them. This is *your* work to do, especially if you are the leader of the space and place. It's imperative that you look around the room and see who is missing. And then ask why they are not present, and what you must do to bring them in and keep them there. It's up to you to see your own revolving door and do whatever it takes to slow it down and preferably remove it. And remember that racism is what keeps the door in motion.

Are You Encouraging Women of Color to Live Their Truth?

Here's the truth. Women of color know that in white spaces they have to be twice as smart, work twice as hard, will be perceived as angry, divisive or problematic when they speak up about racial discrimination, prejudice and or injustice and will often work real hard to speak up about it in a way that is non-threatening, aka *Shifting* (unless of course they are an unapologetic woman of color). Women of color also know no matter how they phrase the racial observations, problems or concerns in white spaces that most white women will be easily offended and activate full blown white fragility resulting in them being accused as the one with the "problem." Women of color and, in particular, black women, often experience what is called *Double Consciousness* while navigating in a white world and white spaces.

W.E.B. Du Bois, American sociologist, historian, civil rights activist and author of "*The Souls of Black Folk*," coined the term *Double Consciousness* to define a person who has a splintered identity. As a psycho-social construct, his theory proposes *Double Consciousness* as a way to understand how black people, in particular, must always view and measure themselves through the eyes of others (particularly white people) to determine their place in the world. Black women especially experience this double identity in white spaces similar to the shifting I talked about previously. Women of color often have difficulty fully aligning with feminism because they not only fight against sexism and patriarchy, they also fight against racism and white feminism. The truth is women of color often have to live double lives (identities) just to survive in white America and white spaces. They have to *behave* one way (the way white society *expects* them to be) in white spaces and can be free to be themselves at home where they are safe from ridicule, stereotypes, myths and white expectations.

TELL THE TRUTH ABOUT HOW YOU HAVE SILENCED A WOMAN OF COLOR'S TRUTH

How often and how many times have you "expected" women of color to live a double life to enter, participate or remain in your space? How many times have you committed interpersonal violence (white entitlement and white fragility) towards women of color?

How to Make Your Space Less Toxic and Violent:

- First and foremost, make sure YOUR space is not predominantly white. If it is, it's a set up for women of color to live a daunting double life. Racism aggressively thrives in white spaces.

- Determine what the carbon monoxide of your space is and eliminate it. Trust me you have some in your space, especially if it is predominantly white.

- What causes the revolving door to stay active in your space? Why don't women of color come, stay or thrive your space? Figure it out and begin dismantling the door.

- People leave companies and spaces because of people. How will *you* become someone who helps women of color thrive in and stay? If you're enacting interpersonal violence, stop it!

- Don't pull out your white weapons (white privilege, white innocence, white entitlement and white fragility) on women of color in your spaces.

- Educate yourself. Educate your staff and team members. Set the bar high for zero tolerance of racism and racial violence. Diversity and inclusivity training is not enough. You must act in the next dimension by specifically talking about race, racism and white privilege or you'll just perpetuate the status quo of white supremacy and the marginalization of black and brown people.

"IF YOU ARE NOT WORKING

TO DISMANTLE RACISM,

YOUR INACTION IS

PERPETUATING IT."

CHAPTER FIVE

Quit Being Afraid to Leap In

> *"All white women are racist."*
> – **Catriceology**

The one thing that keeps people from honestly talking about race is fear. I used to be puzzled by white people's fear of talking about it, but I clearly understand why. I find it fascinating and quite frustrating that many people get their feelings in a bundle when the topic of race comes up. I think you and I can agree that hate, racial violence, and outright blatant racism is wrong. It's mean and despicable right? "Those" people who do such hateful things are horrible, would you agree? It's the belief that racism is this terrible thing done by terrible people that paralyzes people and stops them from leaning in to conversations about race. Do you have a fear of leaning in?

Isn't it interesting that one *little* word (race) can evoke so much anxiety and fear? And the ironic part is, it's not even a "real thing." It's a made-up word by white people that has been used by white people to gain, secure and sustain power. Wow! This get's crazier by the sentence. So, essentially a lot of white people get fearful and anxious about a word *they* created and benefit from; a word they don't like people of color to mention. Sure, you didn't create the word, but you definitely reap the benefits of its creation. Just as I did not choose to be born with brown skin, you did not choose to be born with white skin, but we both must accept the reality of what that means in society as it relates to race relations.

So, what rises up in your spirit when you hear the words *race* and *racism*? Do they make you nervous? Does your guard go up? Do you feel like you want to run away? Or do they beckon you to perk up and lean in? Here's something you need to know. A lot of black and brown people often talk about race and racism. They talk about the color of people's skin and what that may or may not mean for them. They talk about racism they experience in their personal lives. They talk about racism they experience in the workplace. They even talk about racism that happens to other people of color. They talk about the pain, anger and frustration they feel about all the forms of racism that exists in the world. Talking about race and racism is a common conversation among people of color.

Do you talk about race and racism? How often do you talk about it? Do you talk about the color of *your* skin and what that may or may not mean for you? Do you talk about the racism that white people you know experience? Do you talk about the pain, anger and frustration you feel about all the ways in which white people experience racism? Your answer should be no here because white folks do NOT experience racism. Is talking about race and racism a common conversation among white people? I bet it is not a frequent conversation for you. I conclude you probably don't think about your white race too often. Do you find this *strange*, that white people, more than likely, do not think about and talk about race and racism and black and brown people do?

I mean really, why don't white people talk about the very thing they created and benefit from every day? This of course is a loaded question, however, one of the reasons is because "whiteness" is seen as the norm; it's the default, and, therefore other races are seen as different. If fish could talk and you asked them what is water, they wouldn't even know what you're talking about. Water is their normal. They live and swim in it daily. Water is *all* they know. If you take those same fish out the water they will realize they need it in order to feel normal and survive.

The same is true of white people. It's all they know and need, yet they cannot tell you what whiteness is. I recently conducted a *SHETalks WETalk RaceTalks for Women* session and asked the question "**What is whiteness, and what does it mean to be white**?" Each white woman in the room was given the opportunity to respond to the question. Most of them responded with some version of "*I don't know or I never thought about it before.*" I expected these types of answers, however one woman answered differently. She stated that "*whiteness is the acceptable and perceived superior color of skin that undeservingly affords white people with benefits such as power and privilege they did not earn.*" She further states "*Whiteness is such a privilege that you don't have to know what it means or think about being white because it's considered normal, and everyone else is abnormal.*"

Think about that. Toni Morrison, author and 1993 Nobel Peace Prize Winner says, "*In this country, American means white. Everybody else has to hyphenate.*" How often do you hear white people refer to themselves as Irish-American or German-American? It's rare. I hardly ever hear white people reference their ethnicity when talking about their race. Why is that? White people don't have to preface their identity because white is synonymous with human, the norm and American. Not having to self-identify is one of the many privileges of being white. And, while not having to name or claim your ethnicity, you also disown it.

Many white people who have disowned, forgotten or left behind their ethnicity have paid many costs. Many have given up their native tongue and language, traditional foods and culture, rituals and religious (spiritual practices), dance and song and traditions their elders held sacred. Yet, the biggest losses are the result of racism. Racism has given white folks a false sense of superiority; a distorted sense of false-pride. Racism has caused white folks to live in fear, fear of people of color and the loss of a false reality. Racism has caused white folks to live with conscious and subconscious shame and guilt about the horrific history of slavery and other atrocities inflicted upon people of color by white people.

Racism has cost white people relationships. White people who speak up about racism with other white people often end up adding stress and strain to those relationships. White people who are uneducated about racism and lack the skill in speaking about it to people of color often offend them, thus creating distance and a lack of trust. This usually leaves these particular white folks confused. They are afraid to challenge racism and or are worried about offending so they stay silent; their voice is veiled, and they become communicatively stagnant. Racism can cause white folks to lack consciousness of the realities of people of color, often leading to oblivion, disbelief, cognitive dissonance and apathy.

The psychosocial costs of racism are more devastating and debilitating (to white people) than white people are able to comprehend or want to believe. It's fascinating to know many white people are willing to disown their own culture and everything associated with it, lose friends, shatter relationships and live a life that's full of shame, fear, guilt, oblivion, silence, and apathy just to be white. This completely boggles my mind. Wow! Whiteness is a powerful drug! Let me tell you about a conversation I had with a white woman who I would consider being an Ally for women of color. What I mean by Ally is that she relentlessly and intentionally stands up against and speaks up about the racial injustice black and brown people face and fights racism every day. If you want to learn more about how to become an Ally, be sure to get a copy of my book, *Antagonists, Advocates and Allies*.

For confidentiality purposes, I will call my Ally friend, Jennifer. So, Jennifer and I were engaging in a conversation one day about Whiteness. I asked her why white women, who know that white men are their biggest oppressors, do not stand with black and brown women to fight patriarchal oppression. I asked her why white women cling to their whiteness. I didn't necessarily care for her response, but I respected it. Jennifer said, "*My whiteness is all I have and if I give it up I have nothing.*" I asked her to clarify what she meant. She said, "*I know that my whiteness oppresses women of color. If I give up my whiteness, then I have no power.*"

Here's what Jennifer is really saying. She is very much aware she has certain privileges and power that women of color do not have because she is white. She knows, even as a white woman, she does not have the *same* power and privileges white men have and sometimes men in general. She knows her whiteness is and has been oppressive to women of color. Jennifer is both the oppressed (by men) and the oppressor (of women of color). What an interesting predicament to be in, right? Jennifer's insight of her situation is both admirable and problematic.

It's admirable because she has done enough personal work to know she has White Privilege and benefits from being white and problematic because she knows her whiteness is oppressive to women of color, yet she doesn't want to let go of her power and privilege. Jennifer knows, undoubtedly, that she as a white woman has been given unearned privileges and social power simply because her skin is white. She also is very aware that because of the social conditioning that comes with being white, she has in the past been oppressive to women of color. She knows she still has power over women of color. She knows she can racially oppress them intentionally and unintentionally.

I admire Jennifer's honesty as many white women don't have this critical insight and or would never be so bold to express it. Her honesty is problematic because, at some point, if she truly wants to align with women of color to dismantle the patriarchal system we live in, she will have to make a decision about her whiteness. Of course, she cannot change the color of her skin; however, she can mentally release her need to hold on to the "power" of her whiteness. I believe Jennifer is at this crossroad in her life. She's expressed the importance of "releasing" this power in order to advance the women's movement. One thing is for sure, Jennifer is an Ally for women of color, and her daily actions and words prove it. And Jennifer is still equipped with Weapons of Whiteness that she can use anytime.

Fear. There's so much fear swirling in the hearts of people around a word that has no *real* meaning or substance. Race; a word that has been strategically manufactured by white people and used to dehumanize, destroy and divide the human race as manifested through racism. If we, you and I don't talk about race, the manifestation of it will continue to dehumanize, destroy and divide the human race. Race matters. Race (skin color) is at the core of the majority of human suffering and marginalization, if not all of it. We have got to talk about race and racism no matter how uncomfortable it is. You must talk about racism.

What is the worst that could happen if you talked about race and racism? I suspect you would feel extremely vulnerable and afraid. People of color are vulnerable and afraid most days of their lives, and they still survive. I suspect you could be anxious and worried you might offend someone. People of color live with various levels of anxiety every day simply by existing in black or brown skin and are offended more times in a month than you can ever imagine. I suspect you might lose some friends when you speak up. People of color lose jobs and opportunities just because they are black or brown. I suspect you might be seen as a trouble maker if you speak up about racism. People of color deal with this "trouble maker stereotype" on the regular when they choose to speak up about racism.

All of this and more is highly likely to happen to you when you begin talking about race and racism. So what is the worst that could happen if you *don't* start talking about race and racism? Your silence will communicate complicity, which means you agree with all the awful racist and discriminatory things happening in the world and within your company or space. Your silence signals to women of color that you don't care about their unique racial circumstances, barriers and struggle. Do you care? Your silence says that racial profiling is acceptable. Your silence says that Black Lives Don't Matter. Your silence says it's perfectly okay for all the racist stuff happening in the world to continue at the expense of black and brown lives.

Would you rather stay comfortable, not make waves, keep racist friends or remain a peace-keeper, or would you rather raise your voice and risk it all to stop vicious attacks on black and brown people? I hope you chose the second option, you'd be surprised how many people wouldn't. This is exactly why I'm writing this book, to broadcast an urgent, long overdue call to immediate action for white women in particular. It's time for you to get uncomfortable. It's time for you to make big waves. It's time for you to risk relationships for what's right. It's time. The world is not going to end if you speak up. You'll survive! If women of color can survive and thrive in the midst of racial assault, I'm sure you will survive when you speak up about it.

Imagine one of your women of color co-workers or friends coming home from work on a dark night. You hear the faint sound of screaming outside of your window. You rush to see what's happening and see your friend or co-worker being attacked, assaulted and raped right in her front yard. You look around, and there is no one in sight observing what is happening to this terrified woman. You watch as she kicks, fights, yells and pleads for help. You find yourself frozen in place, paralyzed in shock. For some reason you don't move your feet or open your mouth. The horrific rape continues. As you begin to close the blinds, you see your friend or co-worker look directly at you. She saw you. With tears in her eyes, prolific pain in her heart and a brutalized body, she enters her home, and you close the blinds.

What the hell just happened here! You saw this woman being attacked, assaulted and raped, and you said and did nothing! You didn't go help her. You didn't call the police. You did absolutely nothing! You were a silent bystander and co-conspirator to her assault. You were complicit to her attack. You were in agreement with the brutalization of her body. And, she witnessed you in your complicity and silence. She saw you peeking through the blinds. She witnessed your cowardness. She thought she was your *friend*. She thought you cared about her, but you didn't care *enough* to speak up and intervene. You didn't come to her rescue. You didn't help her. Why? What happened?

You may think this is an overly dramatic depiction, but this is what happens daily in the lives of black and brown women. We befriend white women and work to establish genuine, caring, reciprocal relationships with them, and, in times, of racial attack, our white friends are profoundly and violently silent. We yell, scream, cry and ask for help while society attacks, assaults and rapes us simply because we are black and brown. We face these attacks on a daily basis. Our identity, value, worthiness and pure presence is constantly under scrutiny and attack. We face the racial assaults daily. We are bombarded with racial *microaggressions* by people who call us friend. And often while we are being traumatized our white friends peek through the blinds and say nothing; and many times, they are our attackers.

Yes, our white friends and colleagues attack us by committing racial microaggressions on the job and after hours. I guarantee you've committed these attacks and don't even know it. So let's talk about them. "*Racial microaggressions are brief and commonplace daily verbal, behavioral, or environmental indignities, whether intentional or unintentional, that communicate hostile, derogatory, or negative racial slights and insults toward people of color. Perpetrators of microaggressions are often unaware that they engage in such communications when they interact with racial/ethnic minorities.*" This is the official definition offered by Dr. Derald Wing Sue based on his 2007 research article titled, *Microaggressions in Everyday Life: Implications for Clinical Practice.*

I have personally experienced microaggressions for as far back as I can remember. In fact, the first one I experienced happened in kindergarten when a white boy named Marty startled me with his innocent yet alarming question for the teacher during story time one day. Marty was the boy who seemed to often annoy many of the kids in our class. He was a busy body who chased girls on the playground and teased them relentlessly. On this specific day, Marty woke me up to my *difference*; this was the day I saw myself with new eyes. Here's an excerpt from chapter one of my book *Antagonists, Advocates and Allies* that illustrates my point.

Knees bent, sitting with my legs crossed on the floor, with caramel colored skin showing from the hem of my skirt to the top of my white knee high socks, I listened to her tell the story. She always told us an interesting and delightful story everyday as we gathered in a circle on the floor. I don't recall what the story was about on this particular day, but I clearly remember how story time turned into the first chapter of my personally awakened journey and life story. It seemed like every time it was story time, Marty would always find a reason to sit next to me. I don't remember much about Marty, but that he was often quite annoying, and that he served as a catalyst in my awakening, simply by being his annoying and curious self. Marty was the type of person who seemed to get on everyone's nerves; you know the person that when you see them coming and you say to yourself "oh, gosh not him again!" Yeah. That's how Marty made just about everyone feel including me. Not only was he annoying, but he always had something ridiculous or inappropriate to say!

We always got the opportunity to ask questions during story time. I've always been an inquisitive person, and I loved imagining (a movie in my mind) what the words of the story would look like in real life. I can see now how much of a visionary I was and didn't even realize it. I liked asking questions to see if her answers would confirm or deny the vision I created in my head. We couldn't wait for the story to end so we could bombard her with our sometimes crazy, but, mostly age appropriate questions. Today's story ended. Hands quickly went up, and people were eager to ask questions for more detail and clarification. After each question was asked, the story and vision became clearer to me, and sometimes it totally shifted and transformed the images I saw in my mind. I was curious too.

Of course, Marty had a question! His hand went up over and over until he was finally called upon. Every time he raised his hand, he wiggled, squirmed and bumped into me just like an obnoxious person would. I wanted to shout out, "please let him ask his question so he can stop getting on my nerves!" Finally his turn came. Most of us expected Marty to ask a question that was already asked, do something to get attention or ask a stupid question just to be annoying. That's what Marty did. That's how he behaved, always doing or saying things to get attention. But, on this never to be forgotten day, Marty asked a deep, profound and perplexing question that no one in the room would be able to answer, not even the story teller. Marty asked a question that hurt me deep in my soul, moved me to tears and awakened me in a way that I'd never been awakened before this moment.

I will never forget this moment. Marty took his stubby, White hand, put it up to his lips, spit, and then rubbed my skin bearing leg with genuine, innocent curiosity. Before I could respond, smack the hell out of him or push him away, he shouted out his life-altering question. "*Why is Catrice so dirty?*" Everyone turned and looked at me. I looked down at my legs. The story teller looked petrified, as she sat there with her mouth hanging wide open with a beet red face. And Marty, as serious as a heart-attack, looked at the story teller waiting on an answer. Everyone turned to the story teller, and I was paralyzed painfully in place waiting on the answer too.

Time stood silently still, and it seemed like forever before the story teller uttered a word. As I wiped Marty's spit off my leg, and anxiously awaited her answer, I felt like I wanted to run and hide from the world. My mother was meticulous about cleanliness and quite possibly had OCD (Obsessive Compulsive Disorder) about being clean and making sure we were well put together. I always bathed, wore clean clothes and tried to look the best I could. I didn't understand why Marty thought I was dirty. Finally, the story teller said, "*well Marty, Catrice is not dirty; she just has a different color of skin than you and I.*" Marty looked puzzled, and I was devastated! I looked down at my legs again and realized for the first time that I was brown. I was different. I looked around the room to see if there was anyone else brown like me, and it was in that moment, that I realized I was not like everyone else.

Marty just couldn't seem to leave it alone. He kept asking why, and the story teller was not equipped or prepared to further answer his questions. I was six years old. It was kindergarten story time. I was awakened. The story teller was our teacher, and she, although a very nice woman, whom I liked very much, did not have the answers Marty or I needed and wanted. She quickly dismissed us from the story circle and told us to go to our favorite play center. All the other kids jumped up and ran off to the painting center, the arts and crafts center and most of my friends went to our favorite center, the house center. Marty scurried off to the sandbox, and I stood in the middle of the room wondering where I fit in now. My friends called me to play with them in the house center, and, as I hesitantly approached the center, my teacher pulled me to the side, hugged me and said, "*Catrice, I'm sorry that happened to you earlier. You are not dirty; you're just different, and don't feel bad about that.*" I was somewhat comforted by her words but still deeply unsettled within. I went on to play with my friends and eventually forgot about what happened that day.

Marty's question was the microaggression I will never forget. He didn't know what he was really asking. His intent was innocent, but the impact was devastating and everlasting. This is what microaggressions are, often unintentional comments or acts that assault the core of the receiver. Good people commit microaggressions every day, and I'm sure you've committed them without knowing. Have you ever said any of these comments to your friends or co-workers of color?

- *"You are so articulate."*
- *"When I look at you, I don't see color."*
- *"America is a melting pot."*
- *"There is only one race, the human race."*
- *"I'm not racist. I have several Black friends."*

- *"As a woman, I know what you go through as a racial minority."*
- *"I believe the most qualified person should get the job."*
- *"Everyone can succeed in this society, if they work hard enough."*
- *"Can I touch your hair?"*

These are just a few examples of racial microaggressions that Dr. Wing Sue shares in his research. I have had these said to me way too many times to count by countless white people and white women, in particular, in my lifetime. Even before I knew what microaggressions were or that there was a name for these racial insults, I knew they didn't feel right. There was always an invisible assault that happened of which I had no name for. Every single one of these statements is offensive. How many have you said over the years? How many people of color have you offended and assaulted? Are you still racially offending people of color?

This is what happens when you choose not to talk about race and racism. Microaggressions (racial insults and assaults) are normalized and spoken with no regard to the impact they have on people of color. People of color often emotionally die from a thousand paper cuts (microaggressions) per day, sliced and diced by those we call friend or colleague. And even though these may seem like small aggressions, when a person of color experiences a multitude of them on a daily basis, it's traumatizing and detrimental to their mental and emotional health.

Racism isn't always blatant; it's a systemic, insidious mindset, biased set of beliefs and every day antagonizing interactions by decent people. Good people like *you* engage in racist acts all the time. Many don't know it and most do. So how will you ever know if you are showing up and engaging in racist behavior? You stop being afraid, lean in and leap into the conversation about race and racism and expect to be uncomfortable along the way. Expect to be very uncomfortable consistently.

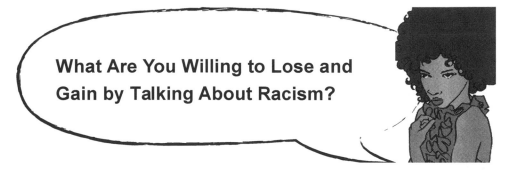

What Are You Willing to Lose and Gain by Talking About Racism?

Not a day goes by in the life of black and brown women when they are not losing something. Racism and living in a white supremacist society means women of color are *always* under attack emotionally, spiritually, mentally and physically. Our existence is diminished, our intentions are questioned, our bodies are assaulted, our culture is raped, our children are unsafe, our men and women are killed, our frustrations are ignored, our womanhood is critiqued, and our energy is depleted by the emotional exhaustion of it all. Yes, we lose pieces of ourselves every day, often at the theft of white women masquerading as friends and fellow feminists.

It's time racism came to an end. Black and brown people have been fighting against "the system or racism" for centuries and clearly we still have a long way to go. It's time for white people to champion the next leg of the journey and uproot and destroy the dis-ease of racism. *What are you willing to lose in order to eradicate racism? And equally important, what are you willing to gain by uprooting your own racism? Trust me, there is a lot for you to gain, but not without risk.*

TELLING THE TRUTH ABOUT RACISM MUST BECOME PART OF YOUR EVERY DAY WAY OF LIVING

If you're not openly, boldly and consistently talking about racism – there's a

100% chance you are speaking and behaving in racist ways. As it has been said, if you're not part of the solution you are part of the problem.

How to Encourage and Empower a Woman of Color to Live *Her* Truth in White Spaces:

- At some point, you'll need to come to terms with the fact that racism in America is a white people problem. ONLY white people benefit from a white supremacist society and racism. Anyone who is non-white is directly and indirectly victimized by white people.

- Acknowledge that racism may be alive and thriving in your space. Look for it. See it. Call it out, and let your members or staff know that it will not be tolerated.

- Then of course, you got to walk your talk. Women of color do not simply trust your word. You've got to show and prove that your declaration for zero tolerance is real by addressing *any* issues of racism you witness in your space. This is a critical action necessary for building trust with women of color.

- You'll never know more about racism than a woman of color, so don't waste your breath telling her or teaching her something she already knows. When she speaks about her pain, experiences or racial struggles grab a seat, sit down, shut up and listen. That's the smartest thing you can do and it's a clear signal that you are *not* going to antagonize her.

- Do not try to shush her voice or silence her. Do not talk over her. Do not label her. Do not perceive her to be the angry black woman. Do not see her expression as problematic. Just listen and believe what she says. This is how you learn without asking to be taught.

- Just allow women of color to be their true selves in your space. Don't expect them to be the spokesperson for their race. Don't ask about their clothes, music, food or culture. Do your own research and learn on your own. Never ask them to teach you *anything* about their identity, race, ethnicity or culture. And if they offer to share about their experiences don't bombard them with a lot of questions. Listen and learn.

• Do for them what you expect to have done for you. Allow them to *just be* without question, interrogation, speculation, accusation, suspicion, and expectation.

• If you are consistently doing your daily inner work to eradicate your own racism and all of the above, women of color will "feel" different around you. They will get a sense that you are on their side and slowly you will build trust.

"IF YOU ARE NOT INTENTIONALLY

DISRUPTING 'WHITE SPACES'

YOUR ARE COMPLICIT

TO VIOLENCE."

#CATRICEOLOGY

CHAPTER SIX

The Environment Is Not Ready

> *"White women's thirst for attention marginalizes women of color."*
> *— Catriceology*

Almost nine years later, upon inadvertently checking out the leadership team of a former employer, they've learned nothing. Today, I was researching women's empowerment groups online to see if I could find some common themes about white spaces and missing faces. In my Google search, the company I use to work for popped up, and so I clicked on the link. Upon clicking on the leadership tab, I saw white face after white face after white face. No faces of color were present. I said to myself, "*same ole shit.*" Truthfully, this was not surprising because so many women's spaces and places are systematically set up this way. They are built on white supremacy and white feminism.

If all the decision makers at the leadership table are white, how does it benefit the needs and expectations of the diverse women who will utilize their services? This is emotionally and psychologically dangerous. If you've ever been in an all male space as the *only* woman, you should understand why. It's inevitable that men in these spaces will *mansplain* to you what you need and tell you what you should do according to a man's patriarchal system and set of beliefs. And, the only way this potentially won't happen is if these men have done extensive work on unlearning their male privilege.

Places and spaces that serve or intend to serve diverse groups of people (women) cannot be created and lead by an all white or predominantly white leadership team. This coupled with denial of white privilege and lack of anti-racist education and training is the perfect recipe for a diabolical disaster. I've been in spaces and places like this, and it is *always* an emotional disaster. It's evil. Unfortunately, it's difficult to explain the danger in this approach as a woman of color because she will be perceived as being a divisive trouble maker, and, if she speaks passionately about the danger, she'll be deemed the angry black woman.

This expectation of having a diverse and inclusive leadership team is the same expectation you would require men to do. Would you be excited about going to work for a company where the leadership team and everyone in charge were men? A place where the vision and policies and procedures were written by men? A place where men are the leaders and in charge? A place where men made all of the decisions and most of the clients and customers were men? A place where men had no clue what it's like to be a woman? Maybe you've worked in places like this before and know that it's uncomfortable and stressful. Well, this is exactly how black and brown women feel in spaces occupied by predominantly all white women along with the added danger and emotionally vulnerability of racism.

Here's the brutal truth. Many women of color (particularly black women) are apprehensive and vigilant about being in spaces where there are missing faces and rightfully so. This includes in person and online spaces. I posted a question in an online community about this recently. I asked the women of color in the group how they felt being in predominantly white spaces. I received varying responses from women of different races and ethnicities who all identified as a woman of color (non-white). I watched carefully for the words they chose to describe their feelings and experiences. As they shared their stories, words like *unsafe, cautious, careful, uncomfortable, exhausting, vulnerable, and dangerous* were spoken.

As each woman shared her personal experience, I felt a sense of affirmation as they echoed many of my sentiments, and a piece of me was sad that this is often the reality in such spaces, white spaces. As I read each one, in my soul I wondered *why* this was so; my mind knew the answers. What do you think? Why is this a common experience for women of color in white spaces? Do white women know this is what many women of color think? Why don't they know? Do they want to know? Do you want to know? I recall working for a women's shelter in the late 90's. I was so excited to transition from grocery store cashier to meaningful social justice work. It was my first taste of advocacy work, and I loved it, but my experience there, much like the women of color in the previously mentioned online community expressed, I too felt cautious, vulnerable and exhausted working at this shelter.

Cautious because white women who do not recognize, admit to and or understand their White Privilege are a detriment to the mental well-being of black and brown women. Cautious because sooner or later their implicit racial biases ooze all over you once you begin to connect deeper with them. Cautious because I've been in numerous all white spaces before and I know what happens. It was a vulnerable experience working in this environment because I knew at any given moment one of my white co-workers would commit verbal assault and cause emotional abuse with one microaggression after another; and exhausted from dealing with all of this day after day. This is what happens in predominantly white female spaces; it's a form of emotional abuse.

And what's more horrifying for women of color, is when white women throw their hands up and say "*I don't know what you're talking about*" or "*why are you being divisive and making this about race*?" Not only is this a racial micro-invalidation, this often typical response has a name. It's called *Gaslighting*. Gaslighting is a manipulative and psychological tactic used by abusers with clear and pervasive elements of denial, contradiction, and misdirection strategically used to make the recipient of Gaslighting to doubt themselves and question the truth of their reality. Yes, when women of color point out the racial micro-aggressions, these are just a few of the Gaslighting behaviors exhibited by white women who are NOT doing their own persona anti-racism work.

Imagine your partner slapping you across the face and then saying you made them do it. Imagine your roommate ignoring you when you're in the house together for no reason, and then saying it's you who is being anti-social. Imagine your spouse calling you names, and then saying you are the one who always starts the arguments. Imagine any and all of this happening to you and whenever you mention it, you're made out to be the blame, and they have no recollection of any of the behavior and or minimize it. Yes, I know this may seem a bit dramatic, but my point is, when women of color experience racial microaggressions in white spaces, this is what it looks and feels like.

The saddest part about all of this is white women are often clueless these psychological transactions are taking place. Let me make this clear. This is not to say white women should NOT burden the responsibility in these transactions. Microaggressions are often unintentional, yet painful, especially amongst white women who have not invested time into learning about racism or exploring their own racial biases. Uninformed white women who discover what microaggressions are and how often they've committed racial assaults with them will be horrified. See for yourself.

Partial List of Examples of Racial Microaggressions

Adapted from: Wing, Capodilupo, Torino, Bucceri, Holder, Nadal, Esquilin (2007). Racial Microaggressions in Everyday Life: Implications for Clinical Practice. American Psychologist, 62, 4, 271-286

Racist Theme: *Alien In Own Land When Asian Americans and Latino Americans are Assumed to Be Foreign-born.*

- "Where are you from?"
- "Where were you born?"
- "You speak good English."
- "Can you teach me some of your native language?"
- "You are not American; are you are a foreigner?"

Racist Theme: *Ascription of Intelligence and Assigning Intelligence to a Person of Color on the Basis of Their Race.*

- "You are a credit to your race."
- "You are so articulate."
- Asking an Asian person to help with a Math or Science problem.
- It is unusual for someone of your race to be intelligent.
- All Asians are intelligent and good in Math / Sciences.

Racist Theme: *Colorblindness Statements That Indicate That a White Person Doesn't Want to Talk, Acknowledge and or Talk About Race.*

- "When I look at you, I don't see color."

- "America is a melting pot."

- "There is only one race, the human race."

- "Where all in this together."

- "We are a nation of immigrants."

- "Why can't we all just get along?"

<u>Racist Theme:</u> *Behaviors That Deny People of Color's Racial/Ethnic Experiences and Dehumanize and Criminalize Them As People.*

- "I love your hair, can I touch it?"

- Making light of a person of color's racial experiences.

- Presuming a person of color is dangerous, a criminal or deviant on the basis of race.

- Clutching your purse when a male person of color is present.

- Following a person of color in the store because of their race.

- Calling the police when you see a strange black man in your neighborhood.

<u>Racist Theme:</u> *Denial of Individual Racism and Racial Biases.*

- "I'm not a racist. I have several Black friends."

- "Why does everything have to be about race?"

- "As a woman, I know what you go through as a racial minority."

- "I'm not racist. My best-friend or in-laws are black/brown."

- "Your racial oppression is no different than my gender oppression."

- "I can't be a racist. I'm part of the LGBTQIA community."

Racist Theme: *Myth of Meritocracy Statements Which Assert Race Does Not Play a Role in Life Successes.*

- "I believe the most qualified person should get the job."
- "Everyone can succeed in this society, if they work hard enough."
- "Affirmative Action is unfair to white people."
- "Black and brown people just need to work harder."

If you've said any of these statements or behaved in these ways, you've committed a racial microaggression; aka you've been racist, and this is only a partial list. This type of behavior and engagement with women of color is not only racist; it's abusive and psychologically harmful to your friends and colleagues. Nine times out of ten, when women of color experience these microaggressions, they feel the sharpness of their impact emotionally. I often describe these racial attacks as paper cuts to the soul. They may seem small and unintentional, yet they have lasting sting that never goes away.

As you know a single paper cut on your finger is painful and sometimes the pain lasts for weeks. Just imagine getting ten to twenty paper cuts on one finger in a day. What would that feel like? What kind of pain would that cause you? It's that kind of pain women of color experience on a daily basis simply for existing in their black and brown skin. And the assault and pain is intensified when they are in predominantly white spaces. Now imagine working for a company for years and experiencing this daily trauma; could you do it? If not, why would you *expect* women of color to and expect them not to "complain" about it?

The expectation that they endure this type of psychological abuse and not complain about it is vicious. White Entitlement, the belief and expectation that white people have the innate social power to determine the climate of a culture (space) who enters their spaces, and how they behave while there is downright racist. There's no better word to describe it, and it happens in **every** predominantly white space that exists. I've come to realize this viciousness happens everywhere, in all spaces even online. There is absolutely no space where black and brown women are safe from the toxicity and violence of whiteness.

I believe online spaces particularly led by uneducated white women who lack social consciousness and the leadership skills to create inclusive, nourishing spaces are the worst. And even white women who "think" they are awakened to the significance of creating intersectional spaces, still struggle with how to manage such a diverse group of people, especially people of color. These online spaces provide the perfect container for keyboard assassins. Yes, assassins; there are a lot of white people who kill people's spirits with their words behind the computer, intentionally and unintentionally.

I can't even begin to fully express how many online groups I'm in that are emotionally toxic on so many levels. White women create these spaces under the guise of feminism and women's empowerment with the intent to facilitate a "safe" space where all women are welcome. And while black and brown women are invited, they often are not welcomed without repercussions. The same repercussions and emotional abuse that happens in real life spaces happens at a greater intensity and frequency online, and the white privilege and white fragility is painfully palpable. It literally feels like a real life, in-person engagement except in real life; I suspect the majority of women wouldn't dare say the things they say online.

So, is it the responsibility of the leaders of these spaces to create, cultivate and sustain spaces where all women thrive and flourish? Yes, absolutely it is! When women's spaces become toxic and emotionally abusive, is it the responsibility of the leader to decontaminate those spaces? It sure is. Supervisors, managers, and leaders of women's spaces must make it a top priority that all women thrive in their spaces. It is not enough to invite women of color into your space and not see, hear, respect, value and empower them. It's your moral responsibility to intentionally, strategically, aggressively and consistently remove any and all challenges, barriers and obstacles that prevent women of color from thriving, advancing and flourishing in your space.

It's your responsibility to identify and dismantle your own racism. It's your responsibility to make your space or place an anti-racist environment that does not emotionally abuse women of color. It's your responsibility to talk about racism. It's your responsibility to educate and train your staff or group members and leaders. It's your responsibility to set a zero tolerance standard and uphold it by any means necessary. If you don't want this responsibility don't invite women of color into your space.

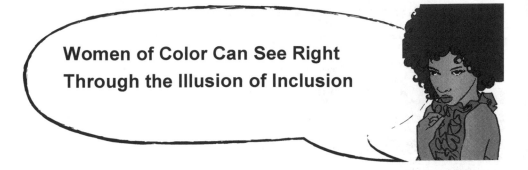

Women of Color Can See Right Through the Illusion of Inclusion

It is not enough to invite women of color to the table. What's the point if you don't give her a chair where she is visible? What's the point if you give a chair, but then do not serve her the full meal? What's the point in serving her a full meal if she has no say in what's on the menu? What's the point of including her in the menu selection if she does not get to participate in the execution of the meal? The point is women of color need to be invited, welcomed, represented, visible, active, empowered, and flourishing in your space, otherwise her inclusion is just an illusion.

TELLING THE TRUTH ABOUT RACISM MUST BECOME PART OF YOUR EVERY DAY WAY OF LIVING

If you're not openly, boldly and consistently talking about racism – there's a 100% chance you are speaking and behaving in racist ways. As it has been said, if you're not part of the solution you are part of the problem. Mediocre leaders focus on diversity and inclusion. Revolutionary leaders know that is not enough and directly discuss racism and white privilege.

Unfortunately, there's not enough revolutionary leaders in our country, especially women. Most white women are afraid to openly discuss issues related to race and racism. Diversity and inclusion are safe topics, but never really deal with the real issues and challenges people of color face on the job and within organizations. Companies, spaces and places don't have a diversity problem, they have a racism problem, and until they talk about racism, women of color will come and go.

A Few Tips on How to Cultivate an Inclusive Anti-Racist Environment:

- *Here's a hard truth.* Where ever there are white people, there is racism; it's inherent. And where there are a lot of white people, there is pervasive racism. Examine the racial demographics of your space to determine the amount of toxic whiteness women of color have to consume just to be in your space.

- As the leader of your space, it's your responsibility to create, cultivate and sustain an environment where all women feel welcomed, safe, supported and free from interpersonal violence (racism) whether it is intentional or unintentional violence. Therefore, you must educate yourself on the ways in which unintentional racial offenses can happen.

- It is not acceptable for women of color to experience unintentional racism either. Being accidentally assaulted is just as painful as a calculated assault. Don't make excuses for unintentional offenses. Educate your staff or members and hold them accountable.

- What are the unspoken rules in your space? What are the obvious rules or policies in your space? Do they marginalize women of color? Do they cause them to shift in any way?

- If your company, organization, club, group or space was previously led or currently led by white people, it was/is built on racist ideas, beliefs and policies. Creating an inclusive, anti-racist (proactively against racism) climate and culture will not happen overnight, but it needs to be created for women of color to thrive.

- Take a deep look at the rules, guidelines, policies, procedures, practices, dress codes, codes of conduct and every other rule put in place on how your staff or members are expected to show up, participate, engage, or act. Do they oppress women of color? Do they silence women of color? Do they create barriers for success for women of color? Do they, in any way, shape or form create tension or stress for women of color?

• Understand that women of color in white spaces often walk a tightrope just to exist there. That fine line is one of wanting to connect with colleagues and members yet knowing the possibility of being silenced and victimized during the engagement. Respect their necessary walk while tenaciously working to eliminate the need to walk it in your space.

• It's a frequent complaint among women of color that they must prove their intelligence in predominantly white spaces, especially when leadership positions are held by white people. Do you instantly question a woman of color's intelligence? Do you fact check her statements? Do you ask her to provide resources or research to back up her claims or statements? If so, this is racial invalidation and racist behavior.

• **Women of color do not owe you emotional labor!** They are not required to manage your emotional intelligence. White entitlement often assumes that it's the responsibility of black and brown people to be concerned with, coddle and care for the fragile feelings of white people. This is a violent lie! It is NOT people of color's responsibility to be concerned with *your* feelings as they relate to racism. Stop expecting them to watch their tone so as to not hurt your feelings, and, when they do by calling out your racism, those are *your* feelings to manage. Placing the burden of managing your feelings on black and brown people is emotional racial violence.

"YOU'RE DYING INSIDE

AND YOU DON'T KNOW IT."

CHAPTER SEVEN

The Dis-ease of Whiteness Is Killing You

> *"White Feminism is toxic and lethal."*
> – *Catriceology*

One of the most challenging feats to accomplish is to convince white women they are severely suffering from their own white toxicity. Blatantly and boldly calling out their racist behavior often doesn't work, but is necessary at times. Kindly suggesting white women wakeup to their active and passive role in racism works sometimes, yet, is very tedious. Trying to provide moments of education hoping to inspire them to take action is *exhausting* because they either refuse to listen and or they believe I should continue to keep educating them on an ongoing basis. So, I decided to examine racism and white privilege from a psychological perspective in hopes to cause an urgent awakening.

Psychologically speaking, white women who have NOT completely woke up to the sobering truth about what white supremacy and racism has done to them mentally, emotionally and spiritually will be HORRIFIED when they do. **RACISM IS TOXIC** and could easily be classified as a mental health disorder in my strong professional opinion. And white people who live inside this racist mental space are willfully caught in an illusion that has robbed them of their true identity, has caused a deep, apathetic disassociation from humanity and has altered their sense of reality. You may think this is an exaggeration, but, if you examine racism closely you'll see it.

The racism I'm referring to is your *every day* racism, and I'm not talking about the burning crosses and radical Nazi behavior racism; I'm talking about good ole, regular "good white folk's" racism. This is part of the willful ignorance problem. White people hear the words racist and racism and immediately disassociate themselves with them because those words usually bring up the good/bad binary, and, of course, they don't want to be or perceived to be "bad." Let's start with what racism is and how the good/bad binary prevents people from taking action.

Racism. How do we define it? The standard dictionary definition does the word no justice and leaves too much grey area. "Racism refers to a variety of practices, beliefs, social relations, and phenomena that work to reproduce a racial hierarchy and social structure that yield superiority, power, and privilege for some, and discrimination and oppression for others. Racism takes representational, ideological, discursive, interactional, institutional, structural, and systemic forms. But despite its form, at its core, racism exists when ideas and assumptions about racial categories are used to justify and reproduce a racial hierarchy and racially structured society that unjustly limits access to resources, rights, and privileges on the basis of race. Racism also occurs when this kind of unjust social structure is produced by the *failure* to account for race and its historic and contemporary roles in society. By this sociological definition, racism is about much more than race-based prejudice —it exists as an imbalance in power and social status is generated by how we understand and act upon race."

This definition illuminates racism on the macro-level, but does not allow white people to clearly acknowledge and see how racism on a micro-level is just as lethal and emotionally oppressive. "Good" white people don't believe they are racist because the definition above depicts the incomplete image of racism they have in their mind. They believe they are NOT racist because they don't burn flags, use racial slurs or exhibit blatant racist behavior. Racism is NOT fixed, but rather a fluid, often invisible and subtle array of micro thoughts and behaviors that cause emotional harm to people of color also known as Microaggressions.

"Racial microaggressions are brief and commonplace daily verbal, behavioral, or environmental indignities, whether intentional or unintentional, that communicates hostile, derogatory, or negative racial slights and insults toward people of color. Perpetrators of microaggressions are often unaware that they engage in such communications when they interact with racial/ethnic minorities."

Hostile. Derogatory. Negative Insults. - The ways in which "good" white folks engage with people of color every day. There's a BIG psychological disconnect between the belief that one is good yet he or she demonstrates hostile, derogatory, assaultive behavior frequently on a daily basis. How does this happen? Racism and being a part of the institutionalized system of white supremacy (which all white people fit into including the "good ones") has strong psychological characteristics of Narcissism. According to current literature on Narcissism and the medical definition of *Narcissistic Personality Disorder*, here are a few behaviors of those who exhibit characteristics of and or are diagnosed with this mental health disorder according to the DSM IV [Diagnostic and Statistical Manual of Mental Health Disorders Fourth Edition].

Narcissists dominate conversations (refuse to listen to people of color), have a belief of having superior knowledge (white entitlement and whitesplaning), believe they deserve special treatment (white entitlement), hold a belief they are special or different than others (not me, I'm a good white person), have a strong desire to hold on to a perceived self-image (white denial), have trouble accepting even the smallest criticism and sees it as a personal attack (white fragility), they have a strong sense of not wanting to be held accountable for mistakes and the tendency to blame others (defense and derailment tactics due to white fragility), they lack of empathy (often don't believe the stories of people of color), expect others to revolve around their needs (white centeredness), and are manipulative (white tears).

If I stop here, its clear racism has pulled a dozy of a mental scheme on white folks. Narcissistic Personality Disorder is one of the top personality disorders classified in the *Diagnostic and Statistical Manual of Mental Disorders* (DSM IV) and one of the most difficult to treat. This manual is used by therapists, psychiatrists and psychologists to diagnose and treat their patients and clients. In my practice as a Licensed Mental Health Practitioner and Licensed Professional Counselor, I have personally engaged with and counseled people with this diagnosis and it is strikingly similar to engaging with a white Antagonist.

Antagonists are white folks who refuse to acknowledge their white privilege and white entitlement and when discussing race and racism show up exactly like those with Narcissistic Personality Disorder. They think they know more about racism than people of color, they refuse to believe the validity of people of color's lived racial experiences, they exhaust themselves trying to prove they are different and that they're a *good white person*, they expect to be talked to nicely about racism and not call them out, and they are easily offended when questioned or their white privilege is challenged and often have an emotional meltdown. Instead taking responsibility for their lack of knowledge and or oppressive behaviors, they blame people color by calling them negative, angry and divisive, and finally Antagonists try to derail the conversation by shifting the focus on to topics that have nothing to do with racism and or they demand to be at the center of the conversation by expecting people of color to cater to their white fragility and white tears.

Pretty narcissistic wouldn't you say? - You can't win with a Narcissist so don't even try. They know everything and refuse to listen. The same is true for the Antagonist. It is a complete waste of time trying to have race talks or discuss racism with Antagonists and you're sure to be mentally antagonized and emotionally depleted. White Accomplices are about the only ones who can make any impact with Antagonists and even they find it challenging at times. I'll share more on how White Accomplices show up in a later chapter.

I wonder if white folks knew racism and racist behaviors are similar to that of a personality disorder would they then see the significance and urgency in "healing" themselves of this mental impairment. You see, fighting against racism and being an anti-racism voice, an Ally and Accomplice for racial justice, can heal white folks and set them free if they choose to be liberated. Racism also leads us down another mental health trail. Racism and racist behavior takes white folks down the path of Cognitive Dissonance.

Cognitive Dissonance is the state of having simultaneous, inconsistent thoughts, beliefs, or attitudes, especially as relating to behavioral decisions and attitude change. *"Cognitive Dissonance is a communication theory that was published by Leon Festinger in 1957, a theory that changed the way in which social psychology was to look at human decision-making and behaviour."*

The majority of white folks *know* racism is wrong and many would disagree with it. However, those same good folks don't see *themselves* as racist and or perpetrators of racism. Here's where the dissonance comes into play. How can white folks on one hand KNOW racism exists and that it's wrong, yet, believe they are NOT contributors or perpetrators of it? These two thoughts are simultaneously consistent in the minds of white folks, especially those who deem themselves good Christian white folks. This conflict of beliefs is closely connected to narcissism and the belief that they are "*different than other white folks and special.*"

This dissonance creates an uncomfortable reality for many white folks. Why? Because when they are confronted with the idea or accusation they are racist or participating in racism, internal conflict arises that forces them to acknowledge that their behaviors have hurt others (people of color) despite their moral declarations of being good, thus contradicting their values and beliefs. When exposed to this startling discomfort they will do one of two things:

1. **Hold on to their beliefs despite the glaring data presented that contradicts their beliefs** (*I'm a good person. I can't possibly be racist*).

2. **See the contradiction and work to modify their thoughts and beliefs to create consistency in thoughts and behaviors** (*I have racial biases. I am racist. I've done racist things. I will work to unlearn my racial biases. I benefit from racism and how can I use my power and privilege to be an Ally for racial injustice?*).

The **Antagonist** (aka Narcissist) will hold on for dear life and traumatize people of color in the process of fighting to maintain their skewed sense of *equilibrium;* because you know a narcissist can never be wrong, right? The three most common reactions and actions to maintain equilibrium for Antagonists are to **deny, defend and divert**; this is especially true when engaging in discussions about race and racism. They will deny they are racist, defend their "*good white person*" status and or attempt to derail (divert) the conversation by shifting the focus on to a non-related topic, accuse people of color for being divisive and an uneducated Antagonist will proclaim reverse racism (there's no such thing) is occurring. And the most narcissistic Antagonists will become emotionally distraught, cry and run away to manipulate people of color into believing it's their fault they feel shame and or guilt (Gashlighting).

Whew! It's mentally exhausting just describing what happens. Can you imagine how emotionally laborious it is actually experiencing this mental train wreck in person, frequently on a daily basis? Unfortunately, it happens quite often in race talks. Engaging with Antagonists in conversations about race is emotionally taxing, physically draining and the worst part is, they don't even realize how toxic their thoughts and beliefs are not only to people of color, but themselves (they're dying inside).

The dissonance within them creates internalized stress, conflict, anxiety and mental chaos which are detrimental to *their* health and well-being. The energy exerted in order to keep up the "*I'm a good person*" facade has to be emotionally and spiritually daunting. The drastic need to avoid the truth and fear of facing one's implicit racial biases is literally too much to bear for white people. They don't want to be exposed as racist. All of this is extremely toxic and I can only imagine what it does to their soul. Better yet, I don't have to imagine. Being on the receiving end of this antagonistic, racist toxicity is far worse and emotionally oppressive.

Why would someone cling to this mindset, beliefs and behaviors? Wouldn't it make sense to address this apathetic **disconnect from**

humanity and liberate yourself from the toxicity of racism? But you see, many white people don't see it this way. Many white people who choose to step up and be a voice against racism truly believe they are "white saviors" saving people of color from those "racists" *out there*. In fact, White Savior Syndrome is a part of racism. **White people don't see the racism that lives within them.** They don't see they are **dying inside** too and that they are inadvertently affected and infected by the *dis-ease* **of racism** as a result of being an indoctrinated member of the institution of white supremacy.

Racism and white supremacy has done one hell of a number on white folks and they don't even know it (or pretend they don't know). Like deadly carbon-monoxide, racism has seeped into every fiber of their being and they don't even know it's about to kill them. That's deep and disturbing! Yet, many white people cling to their implicit biases, their cognitive dissonance and narcissism to remain... a "good white person" all while internally suffering from the very dis-ease they refuse to address, but know exists.

Allies I know personally get it. They understand by becoming Allies they are *not* saving people of color; they are healing themselves from the *toxicity of whiteness* and liberating all humanity. They know their humanity is tied up in the humanity and liberation of others. They know they are NOT free until all others are free. They also don't do **Ally** work for selfish reasons; they do it because it's the *right thing to do* in order for humanity to be free, thrive and flourish.

And finally, what I know to be true from countless personal experiences while living in this black body for almost 5 decades is that White Fragility is vehemently violent. The silence, denial, derailment, arguing, failing to listen and lack of empathy expressed when people of color are expressing real life racial trauma causes secondary trauma. This coupled with the *expectation* of people of color to "teach them or educate them" is emotional insult, riddled with white entitlement and emotional abuse. I'm a firm believer that racism is abuse even when its "unintentional."

White folks will abuse people of color with racial microaggressions, get emotional and upset because they are called out, and then say *"Well how am I supposed to learn if you don't teach me?"* Essentially, they're saying *"let me keep abusing you while you teach me how not to."* There is something psychologically and fundamentally wrong with that, but white folks do this *every* day and think nothing of it. They seem to be completely apathetic about the real and lived experiences of people of color and often contribute to their pain and oppression.

So... let's bring this full circle. When white people refuse to acknowledge and admit to racism and their active or passive participation in it essentially they are denying their role in the emotional abuse, trauma and oppression of people of color. When white people engage in race talks with people of color as an Antagonist it's not only emotionally abusive and mentally exhausting it's **Gaslighting.**

"Gaslighting is a manipulative, emotionally abusive tactic used by abusers to make their victims doubt their reality and second guess the truth of their lived experiences." Furthermore, the narcissistic behavior is loaded with emotionally abusive and manipulative tactics that cause people of color more frustration, anger, pain and mental trauma. And to seal this toxic deal, cognitive dissonance allows them to fight to resist what's glaringly obvious to maintain their safe space of *"I'm a good person"* while abusing the hell out of people of color and preserving their **entitlement** to remain safe.

- Does that really sound like a "good" person to you?

- Does a good person deny someone's painful truth to stay emotionally safe?

- Does a good person lie about their participation in one's trauma?

- Does a good person demand one's silence when they speak up about being abused?

- Does a good person argue with a victim when they are begging to be heard or trying to survive?

- Does a good person watch someone being abused and say absolutely nothing?

- Does a good person mentally and emotionally abuse other people?

Let me be crystal clear. While white folks are inherently a part of the American system of white supremacy and institutionalized racism, this does _NOT_ justify or excuse racist behavior whether intentional or unintentional. There is no excuse for emotionally, mentally, or physically abusing anyone. A lot of white folks want to be safe when talking about race and racism. Ironically, the victims of racism are NEVER safe from racism; not even in a conversation about it. Isn't it bizarre that white people want to be safe during race talks, yet, it's highly probable (unless they've done some significant anti-racism work) people of color will be abused by them during the engagement? This expectation of safety is diabolical. It says, **"Keep me safe while I abuse you."**

To one day wake up to the reality that you are a narcissistic, detached, emotional abuser when you have perceived yourself to be a "good person" has got to be horrifying. And when you digest this truth and sit in it without running away it can traumatize you. I know this to be true for many white women. I have several friends who woke up to this sobering reality and were completely devastated. This is a harsh reality to face no doubt, yet, nowhere near as harsh as the emotional abuse white people inflict on friends, family, co-workers and strangers (people of color) when they refuse to **WAKE UP**.

One of my close friends who is on her *Journey to Allyship* experienced this wakeup call a little over year ago. Admittedly, her sobering awakening has led her on the journey to know better so she can do better. What a difference a year makes. She refused to be paralyzed by the wakeup call and turned her pain into personal development and now uses her power and privilege to combat racism. Today, my friend is a bold voice for racial justice and is well on her way to becoming an Ally and Accomplice for people of color.

The journey hasn't been easy for her and it won't be for you. I was with her when she got her wakeup call and since then she's shared with me how difficult it was to face the ugly truth, identify her racial biases and behaviors and still be a *good person*. She had to face her own racism, call out family members on their racist behavior (and lose some family members and friends in the process), end relationships with friends who thought she was being divisive and create a new way of being, living and engaging with white people and people of color on her Journey to Allyship.

Racism is toxic and White Fragility is violent. It's a lose/lose situation. Knowing this information there's nothing left for you to think about and no time to waste. It cracks me up pisses me off when white women say, "*I'm not ready to be an Ally yet.*" How can you NOT be ready? You're dying inside and people of color are dying right before your eyes. It's time to activate your own personal wakeup call; you will survive it and be a better person because of it. If people of color can survive daily hate, assaults and attacks for being black and brown, surely YOU can survive your wakeup call. Don't spend the rest of your life being an abuser and dying from the carbon monoxide of your own racism. Wake the hell up, set yourself free and liberate the lives of people of color. **THIS is how you be a "good person."**

*"If you have come to help me, you are wasting your time. If you have come because your liberation is bound up with mine, then let us work together." - **Lilla Watson**, Aboriginal elder, activist and educator from Queensland, Australia.*

Racism is Toxic for Everyone Including You.

Racist behaviors include (but not limited to): Hate speech, racial slurs, racial profiling, discrimination and prejudice, interpersonal violence, lynching, cross-burning, murder, vandalism, microaggressions, racial insults, racial assaults, racial invalidations, victim blaming, white fragility, defending or minimizing racist and oppressive behavior, verbal assaults, false accusations, and so much more. Now you tell me what is positive, healthy or productive about any of this? There is absolutely NO peace, joy, fulfillment, nourishment or vitality in any of these behaviors for the perpetrator of racism or the recipient. Racism is toxic, violent and deadly to everyone including you.

If you are actively engaging in and or acting out any of the above behaviors, it's killing you on the inside. Racism and acts of racism produce anxiety, sets your body into fight, flight or freeze mode, creates tension, increases stress which lowers immunity, increases anger and irritability and activates and or exacerbates depression, increases cynicism, causes one to be hyper vigilant, lowers empathy, causes unfounded and irrational fear, intensifies cognitive dissonance, and fosters feelings of despair and hopelessness. These manifestations of racism occur in both the perpetrator and recipient of racism and essentially they sabotage the quality of one's life. Maybe you're not burning crosses or hurling racial slurs, yet if you are engaging in what's called "passive" racism or refusing to uproot your implicit racial biases, you are still acting out racism. And while you may not believe these manifestations of racism are occurring within you they are. **Racism is toxic, violent and lethal**. *Are you ready to stop killing yourself and others*?

STOP BEING AN ANTAGONIST TO PEOPLE OF COLOR

How many of these behaviors have you demonstrated in the past or are currently with people of color in your personal and professional lives to include online engagements?

____ Refusing to acknowledge your white privilege and white entitlement when discussing race and racism.

____ Believing you know more about racism than people of color.

____ Refusing to believe the validity of people of color's lived racial experiences.

____ Exhausting yourself trying to prove you are different and that you are a good white person.

____ Expecting to be talked to nicely about racism and not be called out especially in public.

____ Expecting people of color to teach you or educate you about racism and becoming angry or defensive when they refuse.

____ Becoming easily offended when questioned or your white privilege is challenged.

____ Having an emotional meltdown when called racist or racist behaviors are pointed out.

____ Refusing to take responsibility for your lack of knowledge and or oppressive behaviors.

____ Blaming people of color by calling them negative, angry and or divisive when they speak up about racism or challenge your whiteness.

____ Derailing race conversations by shifting the focus on to topics that have nothing to do with racism.

____ Demanding to be at the center of the conversation by expecting people of color to cater to your questions, feelings and concerns.

This is only a partial list. These are racially antagonistic behaviors that emotionally, mentally and spiritually assault people of color. This is interpersonal violence. This is racism.

How to Detoxify Your Space (Tips from Antagonists, Advocates and Allies):

This is what you can do right now to personally and socially dismantle the real, pervasive, oppressive system of white supremacy and racism. Racism is not always loud, boisterous, aggressive and blatant. The multitude of racism is invisible, silent, passive and unintentional, but nonetheless, it's just as painful, disrespectful and oppressive. You must discontinue the following behaviors and create a zero tolerance for this behavior in your space.

- *Please stop concretely defining racism as people who are bad with conscious hate and dislike and see the silent privilege racism that people of color see that you refuse to see.*
- *Please stop priding yourself on being colorblind.*
- *Please stop bringing up what people of color are doing to themselves and start asking what you are doing to contribute to it.*

- *Please stop wondering why people of color, Black women, keep talking about race and ask yourself how you benefit from being White and why you are NOT talking about it.*

- *Please stop getting defensive when people of color, Black women, express their frustrations about racism and oppression and start asking yourself why you are not frustrated and angry about being White.*

- *Please stop feeling hurt and wounded when people of color, Black women, point out your White Privilege and own your Whiteness and how you benefit from it.*

- *Please stop pushing away, ignoring, deleting and blocking people of color, Black women, when they openly engage in direct race dialogues and ask yourself why you are running away.*

- *Please stop believing because you have Black friends and or are married to a Black man, that you are exempt from White Privilege and racism and understand that racism is systemic and the United States of America was built with racist bricks and mortar.*

- *Please stop pointing out the negative portrayal of acts of "blackness" on television and in the media and pay attention to the buffet of White Supremacy you are served on every media platform 24/7.*

- *Please stop expecting people of color to watch their tone when they speak to you about your privilege and know they don't have to in order to protect your White Fragility.*

- *Please stop writing off people of color, Black women's, pain because they speak so passionately about their struggles and instead wonder why you do not have to speak so passionately about the pain of being White.*

- *Please stop proclaiming that you are NOT racist and start understanding how you benefit from Racism.*

- *Please stop expecting people of color to trust you because you're White and consider the various reasons why they should not trust you because you ARE White.*

- *Please stop asking or expecting people of color to pull you to the side to talk to you about privilege and racism and be open to hearing about it on the spot. Oppression doesn't pause for us; therefore, will no longer pause for the oppressor.*

- *Please stop expecting and demanding that people of color, Black women, make you feel safe and comfortable during "race talks" because they don't have the privilege of feeling safe when racism is attacking them every day.*

- *Please stop biting your tongue and ignoring the racist comments and behaviors of your White friends, colleagues and family members because silence suggests you agree, and it perpetuates racism.*

- *Please stop saying "I am not my ancestors; I didn't own slaves" and instead accept that racism, as an institutional system exists and chose to say, "What can I do personally to dismantle it?"*

- *Please stop saying to people of color that because you are a lesbian or gay that you know what it feels like to be discriminated against. It is not the same and never will be until racism dies.*

- *Please stop saying you are my "Sistah" when you have no idea of the struggles of "Sistahs." This is appropriation of culture.*

- *Please stop appropriating and stealing our culture at your convenience because we do not have the privilege of using or abusing it to get what we want, sound cool and then throw it back when it's no longer advantageous to us.*

- *Please stop expecting or asking people of color, Black women, to explain, justify or educate you on issues related to diversity, cultural sensitivity, privilege and racism. That is your work to do, and in fact, it is racial aggression to do so.*

- *Please stop asking Black women if you can touch their hair and bombarding them with 1,000 rude questions about how they did it, how much it cost, did it hurt and all the other ridiculously offensive questions you ask about our ethnic identity.*

- *Please stop thinking and telling people of color, Black women to just "get over it" or saying that we live in a "post-racial America." We will get over it when White people stop oppressing us, and clearly, and even then, that will not signify a post-racial America.*

- *Please stop saying you're a feminist if you are unwilling to accept your White Privilege. If you don't believe you are further oppressing women of color, Black women, by remaining in denial of this truth, you are living a big fat LIE!*

Denial is deadly! When you deny your White Privilege, you deny a woman of color, a Black woman's story, truth and reality. Denial keeps you colorblind, which keeps you unconscious of the real struggles of your Black and brown sisters. Denial affords you the luxury of shielding yourself from the harsh realities that women of color face every day of their life. Denial helps you actively participate in the perpetuation of racism whether you mean to or not. Denial is deadly!

"BEING A GOOD PERSON WILL

NEVER BE ENOUGH.

LAY DOWN YOUR WEAPONS

AND BE AN ACCOMPLICE."

#CATRICEOLOGY

CHAPTER EIGHT

The Journey to Allyship and Beyond

> *"White Women have been colluding with white supremacy for centuries."*
> — *Catriceology*

Think about this, long and hard. Has there EVER been a time in American history when white women have clearly, boldly and collectively spoke up for and put their lives on the line for black and brown women? Have white women ever collectively sacrificed their money, relationships, time, safety, privilege, comfort, blood, sweat and or tears to ensure women of color had equal rights and were treated with dignity and respect? Collectively, and I mean in insurmountable, memorable numbers, where were white women when white men invaded this country and horrifically attempted to annihilate the native, indigenous people of this country? Where were white women collectively when black women were beaten, raped, murdered and dehumanized for 200 plus years? Where were they? Why were they collectively silent?

You'll be hard-pressed to pinpoint a clearly defined and significant time in history when white women cared enough to sacrifice themselves to be a fence, a protector, a voice or a fighter for women of color. Conversely, you'll find the opposite. White women have often been the biggest and most consistent offender of black and brown women. Yet, many white women will continue to perceive themselves as *good* white folks. Racial justice and equality for all will not be achieved by simply being good people. The disenfranchisement and dehumanization of people will not end with the actions of being good; you must actively, intentionally and consistently resist any and every thing that poses a threat to the liberty, justice and freedom of all people, especially black, brown and marginalized people.

The resistance begins with you. I've shared many times privately and publically that white women have been my number one oppressor throughout my lifetime. Not white men, not black men; white women. And, in intimate conversations with my black and brown friends, they too share this unfortunate, painful truth. During these countless conversations, we examine and question the definition, purpose and intent of feminism. We wonder how feminism has failed many black and brown women and other women of marginalized communities. We question why feminism has been essentially good for white women and not so good for "other" women.

In our, in my quest for answers, I've come to strongly believe that feminism is White Feminism. It was never designed to include, uplift, fight for and empower all women. Its historical roots are anchored in racism and hatred of black women and men, and even today feminism as we know it is exclusive and collectively unsupportive of anyone who lives in the margins of straight, cis-gendered, heterosexual white women. Two of the women's movements founders, Susan B. Anthony and Elizabeth Stanton-Cady, were the epitome of the White Antagonistic woman. In fact, Susan B. Anthony states the following quote during her time advocating for women to get the right to vote "I will cut off this right arm of mine before I will ask for the ballot for the Negro and not for the woman."

And she wasn't alone in her racism and disdain for black people. Several of the early women's right activists were not interested in including all women in their quest for equality. Some of them were downright racist and nasty in their response to the idea of equal treatment for not only black and brown women, but also black men in particular. Here's how many of them felt in their own words:

- *"You have put the ballot in the hands of your black men, thus making them political superiors of white women. Never before in the history of the world have men made former slaves the political masters of their former mistresses!"* -- Anna Howard Shaw

- *"The enfranchisement of women would insure immediate and durable white supremacy, honestly attained, for upon unquestioned authority it is stated that in every southern State but one there are more educated women than all the illiterate voters, white and black, native and foreign, combined. As you probably know, of all the women in the South who can read and write, ten out of every eleven are white. When it comes to the proportion of property between the races, that of the white outweighs that of the black immeasurably."* -- Belle Kearney

- *"What will we and our daughters suffer if these degraded black men are allowed to have the rights that would make them even worse than our Saxon fathers?"* -- Elizabeth Cady Stanton

- *"The white men, reinforced by the educated white women, could 'snow under' the Negro vote in every State, and the white race would maintain its supremacy without corrupting or intimidating the Negroes."* --Laura Clay

- *"Alien illiterates rule our cities today; the saloon is their palace, and the toddy stick their scepter. The colored race multiplies like the locusts of Egypt."* -- Frances Willard

- *"White supremacy will be strengthened, not weakened, by women's suffrage."* -- Carrie Chapman Catt

- *"I do not want to see a negro man walk to the polls and vote on who should handle my tax money, while I myself cannot vote at all...When there is not enough religion in the pulpit to organize a crusade against sin; nor justice in the court house to promptly punish crime; nor manhood enough in the nation to put a sheltering arm about innocence and virtue—-if it needs lynching to protect woman's dearest possession from the ravening human beasts—-*

then I say lynch, a thousand times a week if necessary." -- Rebecca Ann Latimer Felton

And these are the toxic roots of feminism. Unfortunately, feminism as we know it today is not much different than it was a century ago. The *Women's March on Washington* that took place in January, 2017 proved once again that white women *must* be at the front, in the center and leading the way with *their* white agendas and not the collective agenda for all women.

Feminism as we know it is not working for *all* women. So, what do we do about it? Recently, I conducted some informal research during a *7 Day Intersectionality Project*. I invited forty random, self-selected women to engage in a 7 day discussion about race, racism, sexism, LGBTQIA (Lesbian, Gay, Bi-sexual, Transgender, Queer, Intersex, and Asexual) issues and intersectionality. I announced the opportunity online and forty women said yes and were placed into a group to respond to seven questions, one question per day. I asked the following questions.

1. **What is feminism? Are you a feminist? Why or Why Not?**

2. **What do you know about Intersectionality?**

3. **What do you know about the LGBTQIA community?**

4. **What does White Privilege and White Fragility mean to you?**

5. **What is racism? Can anyone be racist? Are you a racist? Why or Why Not?**

6. **How do you feel about being in spaces/groups/etc. (in-person/ online) that are predominantly white?**

7. **Why has there never been a time in American history that white women have collectively put their lives on the line to speak up for and fight for women of color?**

My intention for this project was to gain insight and personal experiences from a variety of women from different races, ethnicities and other varying personal identifiers. I wanted to "examine" two theories: One, *what are the differences in perspectives about feminism and intersectionality between black and brown women and white women* and Two, *would the responses of white women be different (subdued, be politically correct and or an increased expression of white fragility) in a predominantly white group versus a group with diverse races of women?* Both groups were given the same participant guidelines and rules, and as each one self-selected to participate, they were randomly placed into one of the two online groups to either build a predominantly white space or a diverse space.

Once placed in the group, they were reminded of the instructions and asked to respond freely to the daily questions and to engage with and comment on the other participant's responses. There were some notable differences in the responses within each group that gave credence to my belief about predominantly white spaces. For example, the predominantly white group started off fairly shy in their responses, many of their responses were *expected* based on a life time of engagement with white women, meaning they responded in ways that I have heard from white women repeatedly for years.

This included a lot of statements related to them "not knowing" about white privilege and or white fragility and feeling and believing they were not intentionally racist, which is fairly common for white women NOT actively doing their own personal anti-racist work. A few of those statements included: "*This is my first time hearing about white privilege.*" "*Don't people of color have special privileges too?*" "*I don't think I have any special privileges because I am white.*" Not only are these common statements, they are also problematic and signal to a person of color that potentially microaggressions may soon follow if the conversation continues.

I'd say that both group participants were fairly new to the concept of Intersectionality, and there was a collective interest, need and desire from everyone to learn more about the LGBTQIA community, the specific challenges they face and how to be a strong and effective Ally for them. Other points of significance were that most of the women of color did not connect strongly with feminism and did not classify themselves as feminist. According to their responses, they either felt like feminism was for white women or they could relate in some way that women's equality was important, and, therefore, they could support feminism and or identified as feminist.

There were a handful of white women who either denounced feminism and believed it to be white feminism or were still grappling with whether to identify as feminist. Neither group knew there was a second group (predominantly non-white women) being asked the same questions which allowed me to compare and contrast the responses based on group demographics. Again, this was informal research. In conclusion, my theory was strengthened in a few ways:

- White women who have not done much personal anti-racism work struggle with the concepts of white privilege and white fragility and can often become "combative" and or work hard to justify their lack of knowledge and or micro-aggressive behavior.

- White women in a predominantly white spaces tend to respond more freely in ways that are knowingly and unknowingly racist (microaggressions) and tend to uphold white solidarity by defending and coddling fellow white women's innocence. They often openly demonstrate white fragility and other fragile white women often come to their rescue.

- White women in more diverse groups (predominantly non-white) are less likely to speak freely and may work harder to communicate in ways that are deemed *politically correct* thus reducing the amount of microaggressions communicated.

- Women of color are more likely to voice discomfort, frustration and how they are or have been oppressed by white people when there are more women (people) of color in the space.

- Women of color overwhelmingly reported feeling unsafe, cautious, vigilant, unheard, fearful and or hesitant in predominantly white women spaces and some to the point of emotional distress. Meanwhile, white women either hadn't thought much about it, noticed when spaces were predominantly white and or did not experience any form of emotional stress in those spaces.

- And finally, as it relates to question number seven, the general consensus of the women of color as to why white women have not collectively shown up for women of color included the following reasons: *Racism. They don't have to. They don't care. They lack empathy. They don't because of white privilege. They put self-interest first. They fear losing their white privilege and or they fear speaking up about injustice and or do not know how to speak up.* Surprisingly, many white women agreed with these reasons. However, those who agreed often provided justification for the reasons.

In summary, predominantly white spaces are unwelcoming, unsafe and unhealthy for women of color. They are breeding ground for unidentified racism, unchecked white privilege and unresolved white fragility. And, until all of this toxicity is un-learned by white women in these spaces, black and brown women will continue to be unsafe, cautious, vigilant, fearful and hesitant in your space, which means they will *not* survive, thrive our flourish. And until your racism, privilege and fragility is personally eradicated, you will continue to exude the carbon monoxide of white toxicity into the atmosphere essentially harming everyone in the environment including you.

I certainly hope this has been a startling wakeup call. It's *not enough* to be a good person. If you want women of color to come, stay and thrive in your space you must become an Ally and an Accomplice otherwise now you will **knowingly** become one of their abusers, and they won't stay. Hopefully you care enough to not hit the snooze button, and, instead, leap out of your deep sleep to take immediate and consistent action to eradicate your personal racism and become their Ally and Accomplice.

So how do you begin your personal eradication? You begin by identifying your racism, checking your white privilege and resolving your white fragility. Let's start with identifying your racism and determining the role you play in women of color's lives. In the lives of black and brown women you are an Antagonist, Advocate or Ally. In my book, *Antagonists, Advocates and Allies,* I define and share what it means to be an Antagonist, Advocate and Ally and how you transition from one role to the next. I'll summarize each role to help you identify which role you are currently playing in the lives of women of color.

An **Antagonist** is a white woman who claims to not see color; she believes she is not racist and denies having white privilege. She usually justifies her disbelief by sharing examples of her own struggles and oppression. She believes we are one race, the human race and doesn't understand why there is so much talk about racism. Her definition of racism is explicit, and she fails to or refuses to admit to her own implicit racial biases and racism. Her perception of racism is blatant examples and overt hateful behaviors. She has difficulty or refuses to acknowledge the nuances of racism and the insidious ways in which racism can be perpetrated.

An Antagonist is a woman of color's worst living nightmare. She is offensive and insensitive to a woman of color's lived racial experiences. She has great difficulty talking about race, racism and white privilege without becoming angry, defensive, or emotional. Antagonists' are consistently notorious for minimizing racism, committing racial microaggressions and expecting to be educated by black and brown women and becomes passive-aggressive and sometimes openly aggressive, when women of color refuse her demands. Antagonists' cry the most white tears. They are very emotionally fragile during discussions about race and racism, they fail to take responsibility for their actions and will fight relentlessly to prove they are not racist.

And finally, Antagonists' ultimately perpetuate racism by demonstrating the aforementioned behaviors along with frequently proclaiming reverse-racism when women of color confront their oppressive behavior. Antagonists' don't know how to and or refuse to validate a person of color's experiences by centering themselves in the conversation or during a personal engagement when racism is the topic at hand. They are master manipulators and frequently derail the conversation by shifting the focus onto their feelings and needs.

Antagonists' are always operating from a manipulative and abusive bag of tricks that include denial, minimization, justification, rationalization, blame shifting and derailment. Antagonists' are just that. They antagonize women of color at every turn, yet truly believe they are "good people" who do no harm.

Advocates are white women who know that racism exists, believe it's wrong and are conscious enough to not explicitly act out their implicit biases. They may also believe in the colorblind approach when engaging with others yet have a moderate desire to talk about race and racism.

They are not necessarily against women of color, yet their behaviors don't outright show they are *for* women of color neither. Advocates are primarily on the fence about racial justice work. They see racism and injustice and want to speak up, but they are afraid to make mistakes and don't know how to go about it.

Fear is their greatest motivator and deterrent. They are afraid to confront other white people about their racism for fear they may lose a friend, a family member or upset a co-worker. Advocates do not want to make waves or ruffle feathers yet inside they want to. Advocates also know they have implicit biases and often lurk in the shadows attempting to soak up knowledge and wisdom about racism and how to overcome it. They often ask people of color to teach them how, yet don't understand that asking is a racist act in and of itself. When people of color refuse or fail to teach them they often resort back to sitting on the fence. They feel a sense of "*I'm dammed if I do, and I'm dammed if I don't.*"

Beyond fear, Advocates are often driven or paralyzed by shame and guilt. They often feel shame about how racism has destroyed lives and dehumanized people, and, because they have white skin, they experience and hold on to guilt. Neither of these responses are helpful, and they often help keep Advocates on the fence about taking action. And finally, Advocates want to be Allies, but their fear of being confronted about racism is more powerful than their desire to get uncomfortable in order to become an Ally. Advocates are dangerous; they're unpredictable and unreliable for people of color. They are neutral, and, when one chooses to be neutral, they have sided with the oppressor. In order for women of color to thrive in white spaces, they need Allies and Accomplices.

Allies are white women who have accepted and owned their racism and are doing the personal inner work to continuously uproot racist behaviors and implicit biases. They are not afraid to call racism out and or call out people who behave in racist ways. They recognize and accept they have unearned white privilege and are innately prone to white fragility. They have chosen to use their power and privilege to stand up to social and racial injustices. They've done (and are doing continuously) extensive inner work to uproot and eliminate the white fragility, which they know is a form of violence against people of color.

Allies are not paralyzed by fear, shame or guilt, and they take daily action to continue to dismantle their own internalized dominance and perceived superiority. They refuse to be silent and are comfortable breaking up and or disrupting white spaces that exclude, marginalize and oppress people of color. They not only challenge racism on a personal level, they intentionally and consistently challenge and defy white supremacy and institutional and structural systemic racism at every level. This means they are questioning and challenging leaders, lawmakers, people in positions of power, laws, rules (formal and informal), policies, procedures, beliefs, practices and protocols that favor white people and oppress people of color.

One of the most important behaviors for Allies to consistently demonstrate is listening more than they speak, especially when engaging with women of color. Although racism was created by white people for white people and white people benefit from it, people of color know *more* about racism than white people, and Allies know and agree with this truth. Allies know they should never attempt to "educate" people of color about racism and that to do so is racist. People of color on a daily basis fight against racism and racist people which results in *Racial Battle Fatigue.*

Racial Battle Fatigue manifests due to people of color experiencing daily microaggressions and other forms of explicit racial assaults. They become physically tired, irritable, emotionally exhausted from explaining, teaching and defending themselves and can experience anxiety and even mild to severe forms of depression. In other words, black and brown people get (and are) damn tired of dealing with racism, working to avoid racism, talking about racism, explaining racism, and experiencing racism to only be told, "*you're making it up, your pulling the race card, you're being too sensitive, I didn't mean to offend you, how will I learn if you won't teach me*" and a forever oppressive list of unacceptable and abusive responses to racism.

Strong and effective Allies know people of color experience *Racial Battle Fatigue*, and part of their role is to step in and relieve some of the fatigue by specifically challenging and working with Antagonists and Advocates. Antagonists are highly abusive to people of color, and, if Advocates aren't willing to jump off the fence, they too can create emotional exhaustion for people of color. Allies know their real work is to seek out, reach and teach white people about their racism and work to get them to uproot their racism with the ultimate goal of creating more Allies. Allies, just like in times of war, are always preparing to align themselves with people of color when they are on the battle grounds of racism and racial injustice.

Allies don't stop fighting until the battle is won. Allies are always ready and available to support people of color and Accomplices don't wait for the call from women of color. They are actively disrupting racism in every space and place and systemically. Accomplices not only take on the role and responsibilities of an Ally, they are working in cahoots with black and brown people to intentionally, systematically and relentlessly dismantle white supremacy and racism. Accomplices are co-conspirators against racial injustice.

Accept and own if you're a white woman in any given space or place, that you have power and privilege women of color do not have. This is especially important in online spaces where group members and contacts always cannot see you. White women love to be at the center: the center of conversations, the center of attention and leading and upfront during women's events. Accomplices know this *centering* behavior is oppressive when women of color and other marginalized people are in the room. To be an effective Accomplice means to recognize who is in the room/space and then move to the back or to the side so that women of color are at the center and in the front.

Resist the compulsion to center yourself; this means stop doing all the talking and commenting. When women of color are engaging in conversation it's not necessary and often unwelcomed for you to assert your voice into the conversation unless you're invited. And if you are invited, proceed with conscious caution. During discussions about race and racism you are NOT to be the center of attention. Check your entitlement and feelings at the door during race talks and expect them to be hurt during such conversations. The more inner work you do, the more easily you'll be able to engage in race talks with women of color without becoming offended or being offensive.

When other white women center themselves by demonstrating white fragility and white entitlement, Accomplices step in and shut it down! As an Accomplice you may choose to call them in (a nice attempt to detour their derailment) or call them out (directly and unapologetically confront their violent behavior) to prevent further abusive and oppressive behavior.

Accomplices are not silent. They are not complacent or afraid to address antagonistic white women. Accomplices do not coddle white women or fall for their manipulative white tears. They are co-conspirators in disarming Weapons of Whiteness and dismantling racism in every form.

Accomplices directly, explicitly and unapologetically challenge systems of racism and white supremacy to block and impede racist rules, policies, procedures and practices. Accomplices do not walk away when situations become intense nor do they retreat during difficult, racially charged moments. Accomplices often move under the direction and leadership of people of color. They communicate, co-conspire and coordinate strategic efforts and plans to break down oppressive behaviors, practices and systems. Black and brown women do not need you to be their Super-Shero. They do not want your pity or missionary contribution. They do not expect you to save them. Watch your motives. Being an Accomplice is a selfless way of living not any particular set of behaviors you demonstrate.

Check your guilt and shame at the door. If you are motivated by guilt and shame and your self-interests are notoriety and monetary benefit, you are exploiting the oppression and struggle of black and brown people for social and financial gain. Accomplices are NOT self-serving and if you show up this way, people of color will know and call you out without hesitation.

Being an Accomplice doesn't give you a badge of honor to flash and don't expect to receive the "save a POC (person of color)" award. Showing up with a patronizing or positioning power stance is explicitly racist behavior. You don't know more than people of color and you do NOT know what is best for them. Fall back and let people of color lead the way to liberation from racism and oppression. Accomplices do not co-opt the language of oppression, justice and liberation. They do not appropriate the language of the oppressed and call it their own to be "accepted" by people of color (seeking Ally cookies). People of color will see right through your rehearsed justice jargon and deem you an imposter to not be trusted.

If you're not willing to be disruptive and challenge the dominant power systems that institutionally and collectively oppress women of color, you're not ready to be an Accomplice. Accomplices are willing and capable of being uncomfortable consistently and welcome the challenge without hesitation. Being an Accomplice is not a part-time gig. It's not a lifestyle hobby or extracurricular activity to be set aside whenever it's uncomfortable or inconvenient for you. If you want to seriously cultivate and sustain an environment that women of color desire to be in, one where they are safe, supported, and empowered to thrive and flourish, you need to become and actively show up every day as an Accomplice.

Antagonist, Advocate, Ally or Accomplice, which one are you? Women of color may not always or ever tell you directly but they've made a determination on which one you are by the way you show up and engage with them. They're watching, analyzing and drawing conclusions on whether they must stay away from you, keep their guard up or begin to trust you. You may think this is unfair or even prejudice behavior and it's both. It is unfair but no more unfair than the way society treats women of color based on their skin color. It is prejudice but not from a hate perspective but from a survival perspective. White women Antagonists and Advocates are extremely detrimental to the mental and emotional well-being of black and brown women. And yes, it's up to you to prove you are an Ally or Accomplice. **They don't owe you trust; you earn it!**

THIS is the first step to making your space or place inclusive and healthy for women of color. Think about it. It's not the walls, desks or literal space that is toxic and exclusionary, it is the people. It's the leadership, the rules, policies, procedures and formal and informal rules within a space or place that determines the climate and whether women of color will come, stay and thrive. It's you. You've heard it before and I'm sure you've experienced it before, people leave jobs because of people not necessarily the job itself.

Starting the *Journey to Allyship* is critical at this time; it always has been for there has never been a time when white women have collectively stood up for, aligned themselves with and or advocated on their behalf. That time is now and is long overdue. So will you start your *Journey to Allyship* today? Are you willing to identify, own and accept your racism and implicit biases and then work to uproot them to eradicate racism and oppression for women of color? If the answer is no or I'm not sure, please know that any answer other than absolutely yes is a neutral answer and neutrality is toxic and dangerous.

Talking about race and racism is not easy. Talking about racism will snatch you out of your comfort zone. Talking about racism will provide healing, reparation and resolution. Talking about racism will validate and liberate those oppressed by racism. Talking about racism will be the difference maker and chain breaker within the human movement. Talking about race and racism must happen. Nothing great was ever accomplished by being silent or running away from the challenge. Women cannot say they are *for* women and refuse to hear other women's pain and struggles. Women cannot say they are champions for women yet deny another woman's reality and truth. Women cannot say they are humanist and refuse to engage in dialogue that is difficult and challenging, especially if the dialogue is centered on the truth, pain and the plight of another woman. And as hard of a pill as it is to swallow, any woman who refuses to listen to, hear, honor and validate another woman's experience … is not a champion for women.

Look around your space. Whose faces are missing? Why are they not there? Who has come and gone and do you know why? Who is on the verge of leaving and would you know? Who do you not want to leave and how can you help them stay? Should they stay? Will they feel included and welcomed? Will they be empowered to thrive and flourish? Will you be an Ally during times of racial conflict? Do you have what it takes to show up like an Accomplice and lead your space like one? Are you willing to take life-changing risks for the sake of humanity? Being a good person is not enough. It never has been and will never be.

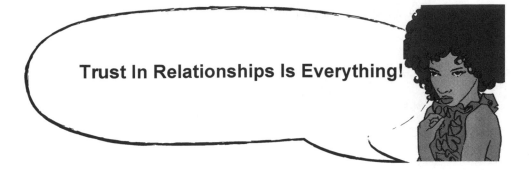

Trust In Relationships Is Everything!

Women of color don't owe you trust. You earn it every day in every moment. White women tend to get comfortable once they've established a relationship with women of color. It's highly possible to earn a woman of color's trust one day and lose it the next. It only takes one microaggression to lose the trust of a woman of color. **Racism is part of who you are**. You've been indoctrinated into white supremacy in every part of your life. You'll always see the world through white eyes and the lens of privilege. Therefore, it will be easy for you to get too comfortable and mess up. Don't get comfortable!

Earning and maintaining trust as a white woman with women of color is not like earning trust in typical relationships. Let me use this to illustrate my point. Let's say for example, that you are someone who has experienced tremendous verbal and emotional abuse for a lifetime. You don't trust people because of your experience and are very cautious about getting into new relationships. You decide that you are going to start dating again and meet someone who has a lifetime history of being verbally abusive. They tell you how enlightened they've become. They promise you they work daily on not being abusive. They have been through counseling and continue to work on living an anti-abuse lifestyle. When you agree to start a relationship with them, you KNOW their history, past behaviors and lens in which they view life and relationships. You know what you're getting into.

WHITE SPACES MISSING FACES • **123**

- Would you expect to trust them right away?

- Would you expect the possibility of them slipping into old, conditioned behaviors?

- Would you be extra cautious because you know the potential threat they pose to your emotional well-being?

No, you would not trust them right away. Yes, the possibility of them hurting you on "accident" is imminent. And yes, you would be extremely cautious as you build a relationship with them. What I described here is exactly how women of color feel when entering personal and professional relationships with white women. They know your history. They know that you think, feel and behave from a privileged perspective. They know no matter how much you educate yourself and or how enlightened you are that you **always** are equipped with *Weapons of Whiteness* to use against them at any time.

Remember. **Wherever there are white women, there is racism; it's part of who YOU are**. So, as you begin to decontaminate your white spaces, the first space that needs detoxification is your own personal space; the skin you live in. This is where you store your weapons. This is why you must never become comfortable in your engagement with women of color. Disarming, deactivating and dismantling your *Weapons of Whiteness* will not be easy for they are locked and loaded and ready to attack at any time. Just as easy as it is to breathe, it's just as easy for your weapons to activate and assault women of color.

Women of color KNOW when they choose to engage with you, it's like walking on a battlefield with the potential for landmines to explode at any time. And women of color do NOT and should not bear the burden of tip-toeing around you. It's your responsibility to deactivate your weapons so they can just simply be who they are at all times. Women of color DON'T trust you. They don't owe you trust. You earn it in every moment. The only way you'll begin earning the trust of women of color is to deal with your own racism, uproot your racist ways, deactivate your weapons and detoxify your white spaces.

You may be saying, "*Well, Catrice, if I'm always going to be a racist and women of color don't trust me, why bother?*" And I say, "*Women of color will always have black and brown skin and they wake up and fight every day just to survive.*" They don't get to opt out and just accept racism without a fight. And you don't get to opt out of NOT being racist when they engage with you. And when they show up in your spaces and places, it's your responsibility to ensure those spaces are not just spaces of survival, but spaces and places where women of color are safe and empowered to flourish and thrive.

There has never been a time in history when white women have collectively put their lives on the line for black and brown women. That time is now! It's time to lay down your weapons. It's time to examine and decontaminate your white space. Especially the skin you live in; the most important space of all.

Detoxify yourself.

Decontaminate your space.

Set yourself free.

Liberate the lives of women of color.

This is what good people do.

This is how you begin to earn the trust of women of color.

"THE WORLD WILL NOT BE DESTROYED BY THOSE WHO DO EVIL, BUT BY THOSE WHO WATCH THEM WITHOUT DOING ANYTHING."

- ALBERT EINSTEIN

AFTERWORD

The Awakened Conscious Shift 6-Point Revolution Plan™

Reckoning | Reconciliation | Resist | Reconstruction
Revolution | Resiliency

If you want to be an Accomplice for women of color, what are you willing to risk and relinquish?

Now is the time for a massive social and racial justice RECKONING. We must accept that our oppressive systems are violently failing humanity and RESIST everything operating to stifle or kill the human spirit. We must acknowledge that our own self-interests and complacency have orchestrated horrendous human suffering and a society that is destroying its own people; that if not RECONSTRUCTED with urgency and tenacity, will lead us into the abyss of social apathy and anguish.

It's time for a divorce. The oppressive, toxic marriage between White Feminism and White Supremacy must be severed if humanity is ever going to survive and thrive. This deadly combination and all of its repressive acts of human devastation must be RECONCILED AND REPARATION is long overdue.

A new, inclusive, radical and unapologetic REVOLUTION is vital to the survival and thrival of humanity. There's significant, relentless work to be done during the reconstruction, and the one essential skill to birth a new, inclusively-humane standard for human rights is RESILIENCY.

This is hard work. Work that everyone must commit to - to liberate the lives of people and to protect, fortify and nourish their existence. Resiliency at the intersection of differences is where you must consciously and vigorously stretch and be stretched to ensure ALL marginalized people are seen, valued, honored, accepted, empowered and protected.

Intentional Intersectionality and the ability to unselfishly and cautiously navigate at the intersection of human differences with respect and resiliency is a non-negotiable for liberation and justice for all. The intersection, the place where our differences and likeness lies, is complex, layered, delicate and life-giving or life-taking. There is NO time to be lazy or asleep at the intersection. Wake up, be alert and very intentional where human life collides or you will create collateral damage.

At the intersection, you'll either be life-giving or murderous with your tone, words, behaviors and actions. You'll either create pain or progress. The REVOLUTION AND RECONSRUCTION is not about feminism. It's about LIBERATION. You must choose liberation over feminism in order to give life. We must become RADICAL, RELENTLESS, REVOLUTIONARY humanists. Rise up, RESIST, GIVE LIFE and be RESILIENT

Onward we go!
The Revolution continues...

RESOURCES
ARTICLES AND BOOKS

Microaggressions in Everyday Life: Race, Gender, and Sexual Orientation. By Dr. Derald Wing Sue. *Microaggressions in Everyday Life* offers an insightful, scholarly, and thought provoking analysis of the existence of subtle, often unintentional biases, and their profound impact on members of traditionally disadvantaged groups. The concept of microaggressions is one of the most important developments in the study of intergroup relations over the past decade, and this volume is the definitive source on the topic.

Sanchez-Hucles, J. and Davis, D. (2010). **Women and Women of Color in Leadership. Complexity, Identity, and Intersectionality.** *American Psychologist*. This article describes the challenges that women and women of color face in their quest to achieve and perform in leadership roles in work settings. It discusses the barriers that women encounter and specifically address the dimensions of gender and race and their impact on leadership. It identifies the factors associated with gender evaluations of leaders and the stereotypes and other challenges faced by White women and women of color. The article uses ideas concerning identity and the intersection of multiple identities to understand the way in which gender mediates and shapes the experience of women in the workplace. It concludes with suggestions for research and theory development that may more fully capture the complex experience of women who serve as leaders.

BOOKS

Beyond the Pale: **White Women, Racism and History**: By Vron Ware, Foreword by Mikki Kendall. Pioneering study of how ideas about white women have shaped the history of racism. How have ideas about White women figured in the history of racism? Vron Ware argues that they have been central, and that feminism has, in many ways, developed as a political movement within racist societies. Dissecting the different meanings of femininity and womanhood, *Beyond the Pale* examines the political connections between black and white women, both within contemporary racism and feminism, as well as in historical examples like the anti-slavery movement and the British campaign against lynching in the United States. *Beyond the Pale* is a major contribution to anti-racist work, confronting the historical meanings of whiteness as a way of overcoming the moralism that so often infuses antiracist movements.

White Like Me: **Reflections on Race from a Privileged Son**: By Tim Wise (Soft Skull, 2005). Wise, who speaks widely on U.S. campuses, looks at his life re: White Privilege he received from age three on. See (www.timwise. org) for Wises essays, collected in Speaking Treason Fluently: Anti-racist Reflections from an Angry White Male, as well as in Between Barack and a Hard Place: Racism and White Denial in the Age of Obama (2009).

Invisible Privilege: **A Memoir About Race, Class, and Gender**: Paula S. Rothenberg (Kansas, 2000). Looks at her life (she is White) and privileges through the lens of gender, race and class.

White Lies: **Race and the Myths of Whiteness**: By Maurice Berger (FSG, 1999). Berger grew up in NYC 1960s with a Jewish liberal father who loved Martin Luther King Jr., and a dark skinned Sephardic Jewish mother who hated Black people: He describes his journey toward understanding racism.

Black Like Me: By John Howard Griffin (1962, reprinted with 1996 Afterword). The White author travels through the South as a Black man to document discrimination he encounters. Grace Halsell (Soul Sister, 1999) did the same in Hispanic, Native American, and Black guise to personally experience racism. These two books helped open white Americans' eyes to the reality of everyday racism.

Privilege, Power, and Difference: By Allan G. Johnson (McGraw Hill, 2006). Illustrates how systems of privilege work (gender, race, ethnicity, sexual orientation, physical abilities, age, income, education, geographic) and how to be part of the solution.

Uprooting Racism: How White People Can Work for Racial Justice: By Paul Kivel (New Society, 2002). Helps White people see dynamics of racism in society, institutions, daily lives. It includes stories, exercises, and advice for working together.

How the Irish Became White: By Noel Ignatiev, (Routledge, 1995). Shows how the Irish "assimilated" in jobs, unions and government by separating themselves from and excluding Blacks.

Are Italians White? How Race is Made in America: By Jennifer Guglielmo and Salvatore Salerno, (Routledge, 2003). Italian Americans describe their complex experiences with race, racism and White privilege.

How Jews Became White Folks & What That Says About Race in America: By Karen Brodkin (Rutgers, 2000) shows how Jewish immigrants assimilated within the framework of Whiteness and counters the "bootstraps" myth.

Killing Rage: Ending Racism. By bell hooks (Holt, 1995). A black and feminist perspective on psychological trauma among African Americans, friendship between Black women and White women, anti-Semitism and racism, internalized racism in movies and the media. The title essay is about the fierce anger of people stung by repeated instances of everyday racism, and finding strength for love & positive change.

Shifting: The Double Lives of Black Women in America: By Charisse Jones and Kumea Shorter-Gooden. Jones, national correspondent for USA Today, and Shorter-Gooden, a psychologist, team up to examine how Black women cope with racism, sexism, and the myths – from the image of hyper sexuality to long-suffering strength – that govern their lives. Based on research garnered from the African American Women's Voices Project, the largest study to date of Black women, the authors' detail these women's survival strategy of "shifting" as needed into different roles, personas, and even language appropriate to corporate America or Black communities. Drawing on surveys of a cross section of Black women, the authors cite troubling statistics on dissatisfaction with their image and their treatment. The authors intersperse the statistics with excerpts from interviews that illustrate how individual women are coping. The poignant individual portraits provide a glimpse into the lives of Black women in the church, in their families, at work, in personal relationships, as the women behind the statistics speak with their own voices about the personal cost of the need for "shifting."

Double Outsiders: By Jessica F Carter. *Double Outsiders* examines the most important issues facing professional women of color (including black, Asian and South Asian, Latina, Middle Eastern, Native American, and multi-ethnic women) today. It clarifies the challenges they face and debunks myths and fallacies about them in corporate environments. It also provides those seeking to learn more about corporate women of color with these women's unique perspectives, their personal stories, insight into their experiences and cultures, and an understanding of their achievements. *Double Outsiders* analyzes critical success factors for professional women of color, provides resources, and offers potential solutions to challenges they face in corporate America. In addition, it provides companies with insight into one of their fastest-growing employee demographics and helps them learn key strategies for their recruitment and retention.

The Souls of Black Folk is a classic work of W.E.B. DuBois. It is a seminal work in the history of sociology, and a cornerstone of African-American literary history. The book published in 1903, contains several essays on race, some of which the magazine *Atlantic Monthly* had previously published. To develop this work, Du Bois drew from his own experiences as an African-American in the American society. Outside of its notable relevance in African-American history, *The Souls of Black Folk* also holds an important place in social science as one of the early works in the field of sociology.

This Bridge Called My Back: Originally released in 1981, *This Bridge Called My Back* is a testimony to women of color feminism as it emerged in the last quarter of the twentieth century. Through personal essays, criticism, interviews, testimonials, poetry, and visual art, the collection explores, as coeditor Cherrie Moraga writes, the complex confluence of identities race, class, gender, and sexuality systemic to women of color oppression and liberation.

Dear White America: Letter to a New Minority: Tim Wise addresses whites' anxiety about cultural shifts displacing their power and privilege— and offers ideas on how to move forward.

GET INVOLVED & TAKE ACTION

Resources for Your Anti-Racism Journey

Book: Antagonists Advocates and Allies: In the lives of black and brown women you are an Antagonist, Advocate or Ally. Do you know which one you are? This raw, riveting and valuable resource is for every white woman who desires to eradicate their own personal racism and become Allies with women of color, specifically black women, to fight racial injustice and cultivate equality, unity and harmony in women's spaces and socially. Become an Ally! Order it here - www.shetalkswetalk.com

Social Justice/Racial Justice Activism & Education Group: *The Socially Conscious Women's Collective* [SCWC] is an online group of diverse women who have passionately aligned to fight social and racial injustice personally, socially and globally. These women are taking action to dismantle racism. *The Socially Conscious Women's Collective* (SCWC) is a global women's organization actively working to eliminate social and racial injustice internationally through education, advocacy and activism. - http://www.catriceology.com/SCWC.html

Facebook Pages & Groups: [search for these groups on Facebook]

- Antagonists, Advocates and Allies
- The Awakened Conscious Shift
- SHETalksWETalk
- White Spaces - Missing Faces
- Femcott Hypocrisy
- GROUP: Socially Conscious Women's Collective [SCWC] – Membership Fee Required

The Journey to Allyship: Reckoning | Reconciliation |Resist| Reconstruction | Revolution | Resiliency: Are you ready to become an Ally or Accomplice to eradicate racism? If you want to begin to dismantle your own personal racism and work to eradicate racism socially - start your *Journey to Allyship*, a 12 month Personal Journey of Eradicating Racism. For 12 months you will be personally guided on the steps to take for your own personal reckoning to unlearn racism and gain the skills to be an effective social and racial justice activist. Click this link for more information. Start the journey here - http://www.shetalkswetalk.com/JourneyTo-Allyship-.html

SHETalksWETalk RaceTalks for Women Weekend Retreat: Join a diverse group of women ready to unlearn racism and gain new skills to learn how to talk about race and racism. You'll learn how to consciously and effectively engage at the intersection of differences to avoid creating pain and collateral damage. This is an interactive 2-day event where you'll also learn how not to offend and oppress people of color and what to do to become Allies and Accomplices for people of color. Register here - http://www.shetalkswetalk.com/Events-.html

Intersectionality Audio Training: Ready to be more conscious and effective at the intersection when talking about race? Learn how to AVOID creating collision and pain when engaging in Race Talks and or engaging with someone who is a different race than you. This 2-hour session shares how to talk about delicate and critical social, racial, religious and gender issues when you are afraid, uncertain and uneducated about the varying differences within humanity. Grab this 2-part audio on *Intersectionality: Decreasing Collateral Damage at the Crossroad.* Once you order it you have immediate access to download the mp3's to learn how to navigate effectively at the intersection. Purchase it here - http://www.shetalkswetalk.com/Resources-.html

CATRICE M JACKSON

M.S., LMHP, LPC

Catrice M. Jackson, Global Visionary Leader of the Awakened Conscious Shift, CEO of Catriceology Enterprises, International Speaker and International Best-Selling Author is passionate about empowering people and making an impact in the world. She's a humanist and activist dedicated to social and racial justice. As an educator, consultant and speaker, Catrice blends psychology, social consciousness, racial justice, and leadership wisdom into meaningful messages that move people into action. Catrice is a dynamic difference maker with a voice that's unflinching, authentic and powerful, dedicated to social and racial justice because without either, people cannot fully rightfully thrive in life.

For as long as I can remember, I've always had something to say. I'm often compelled to speak up for the underdog and about the injustices in the world. I'm a humanitarian, a lover of people and soul who is not afraid to talk about difficult topics or have courageous conversations that matter. Conversations that, if not engaged in, things stay the same, nothing changes and lives are not transformed. I value truth, freedom, authenticity, courage and peace and intentionally infuse my core values into every human engagement, keynote speech, training, and workshop and on any platform I am called to be a voice.

Empowering the lives of people is my passion. I'm on a relentless mission to make a difference, to do work that is meaningful and inspire and empower others to use their gifts for social change. I believe justice is love in action, and I'm committed to loving on humanity by being an activist for racial justice. I'm here to make a difference. I'm here to challenge the status quo, to disrupt injustice everywhere, dismantle systems of oppression, and to wake people up into an awakened, conscious way of being, living and engaging.

Education

- *PhD. -- Organizational Psychology, Walden University - (Dissertation in Progress)*

- *M.S. -- Human Services/Counseling, Bellevue University - GPA 3.97*

- *B.S. -- Criminal Justice Administration, Bellevue University - GPA 4.00 (Dean's List)*

- *Licensed Practical Nurse, Western Iowa Technical Community College*

- *Certified Domestic Abuse and Sexual Assault Advocate, Trainer and Speaker*

Social Media Contact

Facebook: CatriceJacksonSpeaks

Twitter: @Catriceology

Instagram: @Catriceology

YouTube: @Catriceology1

Websites

www.shetalkswetalk.com

www.awakenedconsciousshift.com

www.catriceology.com

Radio: SHETalksWETalk Radio – www.blogtalkradio.com/shetalkswetalk

Hire Catrice for Speaking and Education

Do you have an *Anti-Racism Plan* and *Inclusivity Strategy* for your group, space or organization?

If you don't have an Anti-Racism Plan, you plan to be racist.

I can help you create both. Contact me and let's put them into action before it's too late.

Catrice is also available for speaking opportunities, radio and podcast segments, and organizational training, education and consulting.

Contact Catrice: www.shetalkswetalk.com

Made in the USA
San Bernardino, CA
02 June 2020